# THE COMPLETE KITCHEN

FINDER'S GUIDE NUMBER THREE

# THE COMPLETE KITCHEN

Anne Heck

Cover by Chuck Hathaway

OLIVER PRESS
WILLITS, CALIFORNIA

CHARLES SCRIBNER'S SONS
NEW YORK

Library of Congress Card Number 74-84299
ISBN 0-914400-02-9

Copyright © 1974 by Oliver Press
Willits, California. All Rights Reserved.
Manufactured in the United States of America.

No part of this book may be reproduced or transmitted in any form or by any means, electronic or mechanical, including photocopying, recording, or by any information storage and retrieval system, without permission in writing from OLIVER PRESS.

First Printing December 1974

OLIVER PRESS
1400 Ryan Creek Road
Willits, California 95490

CHARLES SCRIBNER'S SONS
New York

# CONTENTS

I   INTRODUCTION .......................... vii

II  HOW TO USE THE COMPLETE KITCHEN ...... viii

III COMPANY INDEX ......................... 1

IV  MASTER INDEX .......................... 57

# INTRODUCTION

This guide is an attempt to ease the problems faced by anyone who wants to find out "who" makes "what." Those companies which supply kitchen utensils have been located and identified. Their catalogs have been analyzed and their projects or products have been broken down into useful categories. If you want to find out who makes a particular utensil, it is a simple matter of consulting the index. Refer to the companies indicated by the index, and the kitchen utensils will be listed for you. There is also information in this guide about the companies' catalogs. We have tried to solve the problem of finding out who makes what utensils by doing much of the preliminary, time consuming work for you.

Only companies with a catalog or acceptable equivalent are included in this guide. No responsibility is assumed for any claims made by the suppliers about their products or services. It is hoped that subsequent versions of this guide will remedy such unintentional omissions and errors as might occur, and that frequent revisions will keep the guide abreast of the world of kitchen utensils.

Although we would like to list prices, the facts of modern life with its changing prices, shortages, strikes and inflation make it futile to do so. Only the companies can, at any given time, quote an accurate price. The manufacturers or distributors are affected by shortages like everyone else, and this causes delays and changing prices. And even though they try, the U.S. Postal Service is often hampered by large volumes of mail and doesn't keep up all the time. For these reasons, patience may be necessary in dealing with the suppliers during these times.

# HOW TO USE
# THE COMPLETE KITCHEN

The Complete Kitchen consists of two main indexes: a MASTER INDEX and a COMPANY INDEX. The MASTER INDEX is a list of products alphabetically arranged. If you are looking for a specific product, first check for it in the MASTER INDEX. The MASTER INDEX will then tell you which company or companies offer the specific product.

## MASTER INDEX

PEELERS, apple (see also Apple corers)
    Cake Decorators
PESTLES, (see Mortars and pestles)
PICKLING kits
    Bazaar de la Cuisine
PIE birds
    Candle Mill Village
    Hoffritz
    Horchow Mail Order, Inc.
PIE jaggers
    Cake Decorators
    Maid of Scandinavia Company
    Pfeil & Holing, Inc.
PIE pans, (see Pans, pie)
PINCHCOCKS
    Presque Isle Wine Cellars
PINEAPPLE cutters, (see Cutters, pineapple)

Next check the COMPANY INDEX to find out more about each company listed. The COMPANY INDEX offers information about each company, the range of its products, as well as details about its catalog. If the description of a company sounds interesting, by all means write to the company directly. Only the company itself can provide final, authoritative information about its products and prices. Don't hesitate to write to more than one company, if more than one company provides the specific product in which you are interested. In this way you can compare before you buy.

## COMPANY INDEX

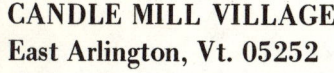

**CANDLE MILL VILLAGE**
East Arlington, Vt. 05252

PRODUCTS:

| | |
|---|---|
| corkscrews | grinders, rotary |
| grinders, cheese | pie birds |
| grinders, coffee, manual | scales |
| sprouters, plastic | |

This is a village of gift shops in the Green Mountains of Vermont, offering unusual gifts by mail. The business began in 1958 as a small candlemaking shop, and the emphasis is still on candle making equipment and candles. A pie bird is a ceramic figure of a blackbird which, when inserted in the crust of a pie, vents the steam during baking.

47 page illustrated catalog 50¢

ix

# COMPANY INDEX

**THE ARISTERA ORGANIZATION**
**9 Rice's Lane**
**Westport, Conn. 06880**

PRODUCTS:

    corkscrews
    graters/slicers
    knives, bread
    ladles
    peelers
    scoops, ice cream

This unusual company is in the business of supplying products for left handed people. They have studied the special problems of left handers in a right handed world, and have come up with some special solutions. In addition to a variety of tools, instruction manuals for left handed knitting, crocheting and needlework are also available. Did you know that Picasso was a southpaw?

31 page illustrated catalog: $1.00 against first order

A. V. FOOD CO.
769 W. 3650 No.
Ogden, Utah 84404

PRODUCTS:

juicers, steam

The Mehu-Maija juice extractor is a device for obtaining juice from fruits and vegetables by means of steam. Secondary uses are the making of applesauce, jam and juice for making wine. Conventional steaming procedures, such as cooking potatoes and vegetables and steaming clams, may also be done with the extractor. A handy item.

Illustrated brochure free

## BAZAAR DE LA CUISINE
1003 2nd Ave.
New York, N.Y. 10022

PRODUCTS:

basters, aluminum
basters, stainless steel
beaters
boards, bread
boards, cutting
bowls, mixing, copper
bowls, mixing, stainless steel
broiler racks
cake decorating sets
casseroles, copper
chafing dishes
cleavers
coffee makers
coffee makers, espresso
coffee makers, Turkish
colanders
colanders, copper

corkscrews
cups, measuring, copper
cups, measuring, glass
cups, measuring, stainless steel
cutters, biscuit
cutters, cookie
cutters, floral egg
cutters, French fry
cutters, ravioli
dough kneaders
dough scrapers
Dutch ovens, teflon
egg coddlers
egg poachers
fish scalers
flan rings
forks, meat (giant)

## BAZAAR DE LA CUISINE (Cont'd)

funnels
grinders, cheese
grinders, coffee electric
grinders, meat, manual
grinders, salt/pepper
grinders, spice
juicers
knife sharpeners
knives, bread
knives, carbon steel
knives, clam and oyster
knives, stainless steel
krimp cut sealers
ladles
larding needles
lemon wedge squeezers
mincers
molds, butter
molds, cake
molds, copper
molds, gelatine
molds, pate
mortars & pestles, wood
pans, asparagus boiler
pans, baking, ceramic
pans, bread
pans, cake, springform
pans, crepe suzette
pans, crepe suzette, copper
pans, fish boiler
pans, fry, copper
pans, fry, teflon
pans, muffin
pans, omelet
pans, roasting, stainless steel
pans, sauce, copper
pans, sauce, teflon

pasta machines
pastry brushes
peelers
pickling kits
pitters, cherry
presses, duck
presses, garlic
ricers
roasters, chestnut
rolling pins
salad baskets
seafood shell crackers
separators, egg
shears
skewers
slicers
slicers, bean
snail dishes
souffle dishes
spatulas, stainless steel
spoons, measuring
spoons, mixing
steak hammers
steam baskets
steam pudding forms
strainers, fruit/vegetable
strainers, tea
tea infusers
thermometer-fry baskets
thermometers
thermometers, candy
thermometers, meat
thermometers, oven
timers
tongs, salad
tongs, wooden
tubes, cake decorating

## BAZAAR DE LA CUISINE (Cont'd)

tubes, cannoli
utensil sets
whips
woks, steel

Bazaar de la Cuisine specializes in high quality international cookware. There is a large selection of fine French copperware, Chinese knives and woks, Italian glass measuring cups, Swedish and Danish pancake pans—as well as every other kitchen utensil you have probably ever heard of, and a few that you might not have imagined. Specialties of the house include a double melon baller (a kind of two-ended scoop), a duck press, and a chrome-plated ham holder. The catalog is attractive reading for those who approach the kitchen with an artist's love for the tools of their art.

80 page illustrated catalog free

## BENNINGTON POTTERS, INC.
324 County St.
Bennington, Vt. 05201

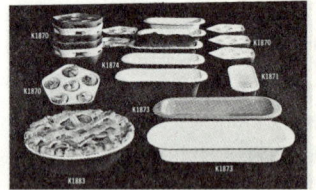

PRODUCTS:

bowls, mixing, ceramic
casseroles, ceramic
lasagne dishes
pans, bread, ceramic
pans, pie, ceramic
snail dishes
souffle dishes

This is attractive stoneware pottery, both beautiful and useful. Also available are plates, serving dishes, coffee services, tile trivets, ashtrays, gravy boats, cream pitchers and many other items. The stoneware is fully ovenproof, but not flameproof.

11 page color illustrated catalog 50¢

**BISSINGER'S**
205 W. 4th St.
Cincinnati, Ohio 45202

PRODUCTS:

    bar units, automatic
    grinder/blender combos, electric
    grinders, chocolate

This company's main business is selling chocolates and imported sweets and snacks, but the few items they carry for the kitchen are very interesting. There is a grinder/blender combination called the Food Processor which is less than 15 inches high, but more powerful than a washing machine. It can grind raw meat into hamburger in less than eight seconds. It weighs about 10 lbs., is shatter-resistant, heat-resistant and dishwasher-proof. Their chocolate mill comes full of chocolate for delicious decorations. Also available is an automatic bar unit operated by a mini-computer. It is pre-programmed for 50 different drinks that are precisely measured and poured when an IBM-type card is inserted in a slot. The last we heard, it was around $1800.00.

Catalog free

**THE BLUE OWL**
**262 East Commercial St.**
**Willits, Calif. 95490**

PRODUCTS:

| | |
|---|---|
| bean pots | rollers, springerle cookie |
| colanders | scoops, aluminum |
| egg poachers | shears, poultry |
| pans, fondue | souffle dishes |
| presses, garlic | spoons, long |
| presses, meat ball | utensil sets, wood |

    woks

## THE BLUE OWL (Cont'd)

The kitchen shop is new to this crafts supply store, and they have some nice things for sale. Their offering in the fondue department is a one pint ovenproof stoneware bowl and wrought iron candle warmer with stainless steel forks sporting rosewood handles at a very reasonable price. Their brochure includes some tasty recipes, including "fresh pear pie."

Illustrated brochure free

**BOWLAND-JACOBS MANUFACTURING CO.**
9 Oakdale Ave.
Spring Valley, Ill. 61362

PRODUCTS:

grinders, baby food

This company makes the "Happy Baby" food grinder, a small, inexpensive hand grinder designed by a doctor to turn ordinary table foods into baby food. With this handy little machine, you can feed your baby the same food the rest of the family eats, thus providing better nutrition for your baby and saving money, since you no longer need to purchase prepared baby food. Easy to use and a boon to mothers who wish to protect their babies from the chemicals and preservatives found in commercially prepared foods.

Brochure free

**BRAUN NORTH AMERICA**
55 Cambridge Parkway
Cambridge, Mass. 02142

PRODUCTS:

broiler rotisseries
coffee makers

grinders, coffee, electric
juicers

## BRAUN NORTH AMERICA (Cont'd)

grinder/blender combos, electric
slicers
toasters, pop-up

Fast, efficient and very sleekly designed can be said about all the products from Braun. So beautiful are some of their Bauhaus-designed products that they have toasters and cigarette lighters on display in the Museum of Modern Art in New York. They have four models of juicers, and their grinder/blender comes with all sorts of attachments for dough mixing, shredding and slicing. They have a toaster that allows you to toast bread slices up to 10 inches in size. Their all purpose slicers take care of cold cuts, cheese, roasts, bread and vegetables. Soft foods like tomatoes or hard ones like cucumbers are handled with equal ease.

Color illustrated brochure free

## BUTCHER BLOCK & MORE
1600 S. Clinton St.
Chicago, Ill. 60616

PRODUCTS:

boards, carving
boards, cutting
bowls, mixing, wooden
butcher block tables

Tables, table tops, Lazy Susans, serving carts and boards and blocks, all made from butcher block rock maple. They will also make counter and cabinet tops to your specifications. They offer a variety of tops and bases for tables in Edwardian, Spanish, Victorian, Colonial and Modern styles. Also Bentwood chairs and rockers. If you have a yen for good, solid chopping surfaces in your kitchen, this catalog will answer your dreams.

Illustrated catalog 50¢

# CAKE DECORATORS
Blacklick, Ohio 43004

PRODUCTS:

boards, cake
cake decorating sets
cake dividers
cake ornaments
cookie sheets
cups, measuring
cutters, biscuit
cutters, cookie
cutters, noodle
cutters, pastry
cutters, ravioli
cutters, tart
cutters, cake
cutters, candy
donut makers
fondant paddles
French cruller bag sets
funnels
icing syringes
irons, gaufrette
irons, goro
irons, krumkake
irons, ostia
irons, pizzele
irons, timbale
molds, cake
molds, candy
molds, chocolate
molds, gelatine
molds, ice cream
molds, sugar
molds, tart
mortars & pestles, wood
noodle making machines
pans, cake
pans, cake, springform
pans, ebleskiver
pans, eclair
pans, muffin
pans, pie
peelers, apple
pie jaggers
pitters, cherry
presses, burger
presses, cookie
rollers, springerle cookie
scales
skewers
spatulas
stands, cake
thermometers
thermometers, candy
thermometers, oven
timers
tubes, cake decorating
tubes, cannoli
tubes, cream roll
tubes, pastry
whips

Over 7,000 items to be used for cake decorating, candle making and candy making. Party supplies and decorations for all occasions. For caterers, bakeries and housewives. Over 150 hard to find pans, over 600 molds for sugar, candy, suckers,

8

## CAKE DECORATORS (Cont'd)

candles, plaster of paris, gelatine, etc. Over 200 varieties of cookie cutters. Whew! One of their hard to find pans is for making Ebleskivers—apple pancake balls. Tender little pancakes shaped like a ball with a center of applesauce or maybe strawberry preserves. Sounds delicious! They also have a complete line of candle making equipment. What a party you could throw making cakes and candles in any shape you desire. How about a cake shaped like a palm tree with candles shaped like airplanes for your friends' bon voyage to Tahiti?

Illustrated catalog 75¢

**CANDLE MILL VILLAGE**
East Arlington, Vt. 05252

PRODUCTS:

| | |
|---|---|
| corkscrews | grinders, rotary |
| grinders, cheese | pie birds |
| grinders, coffee, manual | scales |
| sprouters, plastic | |

This is a village of gift shops in the Green Mountains of Vermont, offering unusual gifts by mail. The business began in 1958 as a small candlemaking shop, and the emphasis is still on candle making equipment and candles. A pie bird is a ceramic figure of a blackbird which, when inserted in the crust of a pie, vents the steam during baking.

47 page illustrated catalog 50¢

**CATHAY HARDWARE CORP.**
49 Mott St.
New York, N.Y. 10013

PRODUCTS:

| | |
|---|---|
| cleavers | steam baskets |
| ladles | steam baskets, bamboo |

## CATHAY HARDWARE CORP. (Cont'd)

skimmers                    woks

Woks from 12" to 28" and bamboo steamers to fit, brass skimmers of all sizes, rice bowls, Chinese spoons and oriental cooking utensils of all kinds. They have discontinued their catalog due to rapid price changes recently. They are included here even so, as they have an extensive variety of hard to find utensils. If you do like oriental kitchenware, try writing to inquire about availability and price of particular items you wish to purchase.

No catalog

## CHEMEX CORP.
505 East St.
Pittsfield, Mass. 01201

PRODUCTS:

    coffee makers
    water kettles, glass

Well known manufacturers of hand blown, filter drip method coffee makers. They also manufacture filter papers and accessories such as grids for using the glass water kettles on electric ranges. Catalog has detailed instructions on brewing coffee their way. The coffee maker and water kettle are on display in the Smithsonian Institute as examples of uniqueness and beauty of design.

Illustrated catalog free

**CLEAN WATER SOCIETY**
706 Chase Ave.
West Palm Beach, Fla. 33401

PRODUCTS:
water distillers

These are portable water distillers that plug in. The water is fed into the distillers manually, and there are no special plumbing or electrical hookups. Of the four models available, three are self-sterilizing, and two are completely automatic. None of these distillers uses chemicals or filters; the distillation is completely electric. The four models vary in capacity. The largest can distill 14 gallons of water in 24 hours; two models have a capacity of eight gallons, and the smallest has a capacity of four gallons. These machines are intended for the removal of all chemicals, minerals and impurities from tap water for the purposes of drinking and cooking.

Illustrated brochure free

**CORNWALL CORPORATION**
500 Harrison Ave.
Boston, Mass. 02118

PRODUCTS:

| | |
|---|---|
| broilers, electric | ice cream freezers, electric, manual |
| can openers | oven/broilers |
| casseroles, electric | pans, fondue, electric |
| coffee makers | popcorn poppers |
| friers, deep fat, electric | woks, electric |

Cornwall is engaged in the manufacture and sale of kitchen electrics. They offer a broad line of food-warming trays that includes a hot cart and a combination tray/TV table, hot servers and bun warmers for use at the table, table stoves, hot plates and tabletop ranges. Their electric wok doubles as a tempura cooker—a good appliance for the gourmet oriental cook.

Color illustrated catalog free

# CROSS IMPORTS, INC.
210 Hanover St.
Boston, Mass. 02113

PRODUCTS:

apple corers
basters, nylon
boards, cutting
bowls, mixing, stainless steel
butter curlers
cake decorating sets
can openers
clam/oyster openers
clam steamers
cleavers
coffee makers
coffee makers, espresso
coffee makers, Turkish
colanders
cookie sheets
corks
corkscrews
cups, baba rhum
cups, measuring, stainless steel
cutters, cake
cutters, cole slaw
cutters, cookie
cutters, French fry
cutters, noodle
cutters, pastry
cutters, ravioli
dough kneaders
Dutch ovens, cast iron
Dutch ovens, cast iron enameled
egg poachers
flan rings
forks, fondue
forks, meat (giant)

forks, snail
friers, deep fat, top of stove
griddles, aluminum
griddles, cast iron
grinders, cheese
grinders, coffee
grinders, electric
grinders, fruit
grinders, meat, manual
grinders, nutmeg
grinders, rotary
grinders, salt/pepper
grinders, sausage
grinders, universal
irons, krumkake
irons, pizzelle
irons, timbale
jar openers
juicers
knife sharpeners, butcher's steel
knives, bread
knives, carbon steel
knives, clam/oyster
ladles
larding needles
meat saws
molds, cake
molds, cookie
molds, gelatine
molds, ice cream
molds, pate
mortars & pestles, wood
noodle making machines

# CROSS IMPORTS, INC. (Cont'd)

pans, asparagus boiler
pans, baking
pans, bread
pans, broiler
pans, cake
pans, cake, springform
pans, crepe suzette
pans, double boiler
pans, ebelskiver
pans, enameled cast iron
pans, fish boiler
pans, fondue
pans, fry
pans, fry, aluminum
pans, fry, cast iron
pans, fry, teflon
pans, muffin
pans, omelet
pans, omelet, cast iron
pans, pie
pans, pizza
pans, roasting
pans, sauce
pans, tart
pastry brushes
peelers
popcorn poppers
poultry lifters
presses, burger
presses, cookie
presses, garlic
rice steamers
ricers
roasting racks
rollers, pastry
rollers, ravioli

rolling pins
salad baskets
sausage stuffers
scales
scoops, ice cream
seafood shell crackers
shrimp shellers
sifters
skewers
skillets
skillets, cast iron
skillets, partitioned
skimmers
slicers
slicers, cheese
snail dishes
spaetzle machines
spatulas
spatulas, stainless steel
spatulas, wood
spoons, measuring
spoons, mixing
steak hammers
steam baskets
stock pots
strainers, extra fine mesh
strainers, fruit/vegetable
strainers, tea
strainers, tomato
tea infusers
thermometers, candy
thermometers, freezer/
   refrigerator
thermometers, meat
thermometers, oven
toasters, sandwich

# CROSS IMPORTS, INC. (Cont'd)

tongs
tongs, ice
tongs, salad
tongs, snail
tubes, cake decorating
tubes, cannoli
tubes, cream roll
tubes, pastry
utensil sets, wood
vegetable choppers
waffle irons, top of stove
water kettles, enamel
whips
whisks
woks, steel

Cross Imports sells unusual, difficult to find, quality cooking and baking utensils from France, Italy, Germany and America. Very good lines of heavy duty aluminum, stainless, cast iron and enameled cast iron cookwares. A variety of large and small strainers and colanders with handles to help you make soup stocks, sauces, spaghetti or salads. Spin-dry salad baskets from France to crisp your lettuce. All sizes and shapes of carbon steel knives of professional quality. Many cherry wood and beech wood forks, batter spoons, ladles, spatulas and other useful mixing utensils. As you can see from the product list, they have all you need to be a gourmet cook. Their catalog includes many delicious recipes to get you going. Good quality, extensive variety, reasonable prices are what you find at Cross Imports, Inc.

Illustrated catalog 25¢

## CUMBERLAND ASSOCIATES
P.O. Box 868
Collegedale, Tenn. 37315

PRODUCTS:

water distillers

Ocean liners and hospitals have been making their own pure water for a while. Now that water pollution is so widespread, the need for a water purifier/distiller for the home is growing.

## CUMBERLAND ASSOCIATES (Cont'd)

100% pure water can only be obtained through steam distillation. These home distillers remove fluoride, chlorine, iron, nitrates, nitrites, inorganic minerals, chemicals, poisons and bacteria from your drinking water. This company distributes five different models ranging in size from 14 gallons to four gallons of distilled water every 24 hours.

Illustrated brochure free

## DAISYFRESH YOGURT COMPANY
P.O. Box 36
Santa Cruz, Calif. 95063

PRODUCTS:

    kitchen heat pads
    yogurt making equipment

Equipment for making your own yogurt. Home or restaurant size. One of the items, an electric heating pad, is useful for other jobs, like making sprouts and raising dough. Their Bulgarian yogurt culture makes a yogurt more like sour cream than commercial yogurt. Free brochure has helpful yogurt making hints and recipes. One is for yogurt popsicles. Yummy!

Brochure free

## E. DeHILLERIN
18-20 Rue Coquilliere
Paris 1er, France

PRODUCTS:

casseroles
casseroles, copper
cleavers
colanders
cutters, cookie

## E. De HILLERIN (Cont'd)

cutters, French fry
cutters, pastry
Dutch ovens
flan rings
funnels
griddles, top of stove
grinders, salt/pepper
grinders, universal
juicers
knives, carbon steel
meat saws
molds, cake
molds, chocolate
molds, gelatine
molds, pate
pans, fish boiler
pans, fondue
pans, fry, copper
pans, omelet
pans, sauce
pans, sauce, copper
pastry brushes
presses, duck
rollers, docker
salad baskets
scales
scoops, ice cream
spatulas
stock pots
strainers, fruit/vegetable
tubes, pastry
utensil sets, stainless steel
whips
whippers, charger

There's more to this company than the product list tells, but the catalog is in French and I'm not too sure what to call some things. Of course their line of copper cookware is superb and the duck press is a sight to behold and the scales are very nice—the old fashioned kind with separate weights. It's very interesting to look through this catalog and see how design varies from what you're used to seeing from American companies. Do ask for an American price list if you order the catalog.

Illustrated catalog

**DHARMA PRODUCTS**
6505 57th Ave. S.
Seattle, Wash. 98118

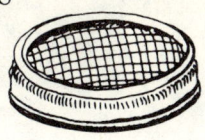 

PRODUCTS:

sprouter lids

These are screened lids for sprouting seeds in wide mouthed Mason jars. They come in sets of three graded lids, for sprouting everything from chia seeds to mung beans. The two basic sets are called "Sprout-Ease" and "Econo-Sprouter," and differ only in the fact that the "Sprout-Ease" package contains samples of alfalfa, wheat and mung beans, while the "Econo-Sprouter" does not include samples. This is a very simple idea, but a very inexpensive and easy way to increase the vitamin intake of your family. Soybeans, for instance, undergo a 553% increase in vitamin C while sprouting. All this from just seeds, water and air. This is an excellent nutritional investment.

6 page illustrated brochure free

**EMPIRE COFFEE & TEA CO.**
486 Ninth Ave.
New York, N.Y. 10018

PRODUCTS:

| | |
|---|---|
| coffee makers | grinders, coffee, electric |
| coffee makers, espresso | grinders, coffee, manual |
| coffee makers, Turkish | grinders, salt/pepper |

This company offers a very extensive variety of coffees, teas and spices. Their coffee makers come in many sizes and varieties, including automatic electric drip types. Their prices are competitive, and whether you're a coffee connoisseur or just beginning to experiment, this catalog is exotic enough to hold your interest.

Catalog free

## FASHIONABLE
Rocky Hill, N.J. 08553

PRODUCTS:

bakers, top of stove
basters, stainless steel
boards, cutting
bowls, mixing, stainless steel
casseroles, aluminum
pans, broiler
peelers
skillets, partitioned
utensil sets

This company offers specially constructed items for people who are handicapped, particularly those without the use of one of their arms or hands; for example: mixing bowls with handles, cutting boards with nails to hold vegetables for slicing. Boards have suction cups to anchor them.

22 page illustrated catalog 25¢

## FINLAND DESIGN, INC.
816 Lancaster Ave.
Bryn Mawr, Penn. 19010

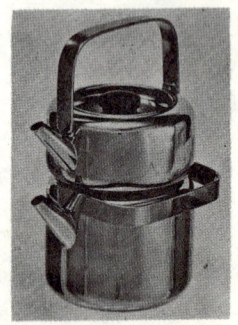

PRODUCTS:

casseroles, stainless steel
pans, fondue
pans, sauce, stainless steel
water kettles, stainless steel

High quality stainless steel utensils designed in Finland. Original designs by Timo Sarpaneva stress good materials and pleasing forms. A 3 mm aluminum layer is sprayed on the bottom of the pots and pans, then turned and ground, so that heat is conducted faster and evenly.

Color illustrated brochure free

## FORREST JONES, INC.
3274 Sacramento St.
San Francisco, Calif. 94115

PRODUCTS:

boards, cutting
butcher block tables
casseroles, ceramic
spoons, mixing
corkscrews
knives, stainless steel
pans, enameled cast iron

This store carries "everything" for the kitchen and some service pieces and accessories for the dining room and bar. In many cases they seek the most inexpensive sources as long as the items actually do what they're supposed to do without breaking. On the other hand, much of the cookware is expensive brands, such as Le Creuset iron enamelware and Spring Brothers copperware. Durability and esthetics are the guideline. They offer a complete selection of cutting boards and John Boas butcher block work tables. One unusual service they offer is guidance in buying restaurant equipment for the home. If you're in the Bay Area, drop in. They have a restaurant stove installed for customers to try out. The store opened in the spring of 1974 and, as we go to press, has no catalog, but write them anyway—they may have one soon.

## GENERAL NUTRITION CORP.
921 Penn Ave.
Pittsburgh, Penn. 15222

PRODUCTS:

Dutch ovens, stainless steel
grinders, grain
juicers
pans, sauce, stainless steel
skillets, cast iron
water filters
water purifiers
yogurt making equipment

The main business of this company is mail-order vitamins and diet supplements. They have an extensive catalog of natural

## GENERAL NUTRITION CORP. (Cont'd)

products, including honey and vegetable oils. The few kitchen utensils in their line are of good quality and reasonably priced. If you live in a town that doesn't have a health food store, you may mail-order from this company many items you can't find in your local supermarket.

Catalog free

## GREEK ISLAND LTD.
215 East 49th St.
New York, N.Y.

PRODUCTS:

casseroles, copper          coffee makers, Turkish

As the name implies, this company imports a wide variety of Greek products, including records and tapes recorded in Greece. Besides the tin-lined, hand hammered copper casseroles and coffee makers, they have Greek coffee, baskets and pottery. Lots of nice things like pictures and pitchers to decorate your kitchen, too, and beautiful Greek clothes to decorate you.

Illustrated catalog free

## HOFFRITZ
20 Cooper Square
New York, N.Y. 10003

PRODUCTS:

boards, carving
boards, cheese
boards, cutting
butter curlers
can openers
clam/oyster openers

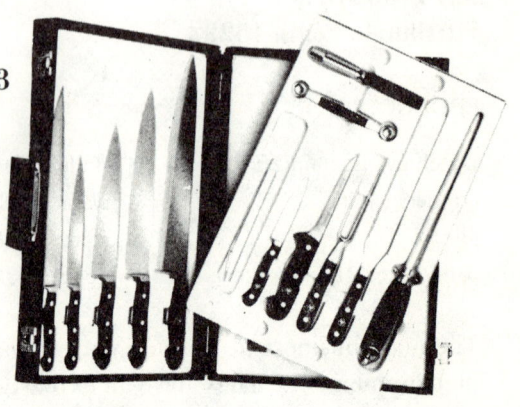

# HOFFRITZ (Cont'd)

- cleavers
- coffee makers, espresso
- corkscrews
- cups, measuring, stainless steel
- cutters, cookie
- egg coddlers
- egg poachers
- egg separators
- forks, fondue
- forks, snail
- grills, fish
- grinders, nutmeg
- grinders, salt/pepper
- juicers
- knife/fork combos
- knife sharpeners
- knife sharpeners, butcher's steel
- knives, bread
- knives, cake
- knives, carbon steel
- knives, clam/oyster
- knives, stainless steel
- mincers
- mortars & pestles, brass
- nutcrackers
- peelers
- pie birds
- pitters, cherry
- presses, burger
- scales
- scoops, ice cream
- scoops, wooden
- seafood shell crackers
- shears
- shears, poultry
- skewers
- slicers, cheese
- snail dishes
- spatulas, stainless steel
- steak hammers
- steam baskets
- strainers, pan
- tea infusers
- timers
- tongs
- tongs, ice
- tongs, salad
- tongs, snail
- tongs, wooden
- utensil sets
- utensil sets, stainless steel
- utensil sets, wood
- water kettles, brass
- water kettles, copper

Hoffritz is probably the most famous store in the world for cutlery. They feature Sabatier French knives for the kitchen, as well as hunting knives, Swiss Army knives, pocket knives and manicure equipment. Also sewing and barber's scissors and tools. Their kitchen gadgets and bar accessories are beautifully designed, elegant as well as useful. If you are fond of snails, lobsters, clams, oysters or eggs, they have all the special tools you need to cook and eat them gracefully. Also barbe-

## HOFFRITZ (Cont'd)

cue and picnic utensils. While most of their goods cost more than you'd pay for something similar in your neighborhood hardware store, the superior quality makes them a bargain in the long run.

48 page color illustrated catalog $1.00


## HOLLAND HANDICRAFTS
Pruimendijk 24
Rijsoord, Holland

PRODUCTS:

boards, cheese
boards, cookie
cheese forms
molds, butter
molds, chocolate
molds, cookie

Hand carved wooden molds and story-book metal molds, cookie boards, butter molds, all right out of a fairytale. These are beautiful items collected by American Adrienne Trouw. Recipes and instructions are included with your order. The best policy would be to send your request airmail.

Illustrated brochure $1.00

**HOMESTEAD INDUSTRIES**
2014 Los Angeles Ave.
Berkeley, Calif. 94707
and
General Delivery
Argenta, B.C.
Canada

PRODUCTS:

| | |
|---|---|
| bottle cappers | ice cream freezers, electric |
| churns, electric | ice cream freezers, manual |
| dough kneaders | juicers |
| Dutch ovens, stainless steel | pans, fry, stainless steel |
| grinders, grain | pans, sauce, stainless steel |
| grinders, grain, stone | sausage stuffers |
| grinders, meat, electric | strainers, fruit/vegetable |

This is a company with a strong philosophy. It is their belief that the dehumanization that accompanies the development of large scale technology can only be counteracted by the growth of local, independent economies. The tools they offer are selected with this goal in mind. They provide tools with which you can do many things that will lead you in a self-sufficient direction. They are all for growing your own food, grinding your own flour, juicing your own fruits and vegetables. Their grain mills come in five models, ranging from a deluxe version, which is comparable with the best on the market, to a stripped-down grinding mechanism for which you must supply your own motor. Also available is the "Biko-Generator," a means of converting your leg power into electricity.

Illustrated brochures free
Illustrated catalog $1.00 (includes $2.00 credit on first order)

**HORCHOW MAIL ORDER, INC.**
4435 Simonton Road
Dallas, Tex. 75240

PRODUCTS:

boards, carving
boards, cutting
casseroles
cleavers
coffee makers
coffee makers, espresso
colanders, copper
egg coddlers
egg poachers
forks, salad serving
forks, snail
grinders, salt/pepper
knives, stainless steel
noodle making machines
pans, asparagus boiler
pans, crepe suzette
pans, double boiler, copper
pans, fish boiler
pans, lasagne
pans, omelet
pans, sauce, copper
pans, sauce, glass
pie birds
rice balls
scales
scoops, ice cream
seafood shell crackers
shears, poultry
slicers, cheese
snail dishes
souffle dishes
steam baskets
tea infusers
timers
tongs
tongs, small
whisks
woks, steel

High quality gift items ranging from $5.00 to $700.00. Many exclusive and imported items. They have a copper double boiler with white porcelain liner for sauces that can't be prepared in metal pans. Expensive but beautiful. They have more than one catalog and emphasize high fashion merchandise for entertaining at home.

1 year catalog subscription (6 catalogs) $1.00

**JUICE MASTER
   MANUFACTURING CO.**
407 Franklin St.
Peoria, Ill. 61602

PRODUCTS:

   juicers

This company manufactures the Atlas King centrifugal juicer. This is a high quality, heavy duty machine that is capable of juicing just about anything that can be juiced. Carrots, oranges, berries, apples, spinach, celery, pineapples—just slice them into chunks that can be pushed down the slot and watch them dribble out the spout a few seconds later. The secret is a heavy duty cutter blade that spins at 3,400 to 3,600 revolutions per minute. Cleaning the machine is facilitated by special paper-like filters made of vegetable fiber that trap the residue and are easily removed and disposed of. The Atlas King juicer is equipped with a motor that runs on standard current and never requires oiling or greasing. The machine carries a lifetime guarantee against defects in materials or workmanship. This juicer is a major addition to any kitchen.

Illustrated brochure free

**LEE ENGINEERING CO.**
**2023 West Wisconsin Ave.**
**Milwaukee, Wisc. 53201**

PRODUCTS:

   grinders, grain, stone

These mills grind grain for flour or cereal. All electric, powered by Lee Universal Motors, which were designed originally for aircraft use. As a result their output is maximum for a minimum amount of weight. Horsepower is about four times

# LEE ENGINEERING CO. (Cont'd)

that of other motors of equivalent dimensions. They operate on the attrition principle. Grain is abraded to flour by the centrifugal action forcing it against a stationary stone ring. The grinding stone is carborundum, which is second only to diamonds in hardness and never requires redressing. Their home mills are fully automatic and are available in four models. They also have larger mills for commercial use and special laboratory models.

Illustrated brochure free

## THE LEFT HAND
145 East 27th St.
New York, N.Y. 10016

PRODUCTS:

boards, cheese
corkscrews
cups, measuring
knife/fork combos
knives, cake
knives, stainless steel
ladles
peelers
scoops, ice cream
spoons, mustache

A wholesale and retail company dealing exclusively in products for left handed people. They have lots of things besides kitchen utensils, like left-handed baseball mitts, left-handed golf clubs and left-handed scissors. In the kitchen department, their corkscrew spirals counter-clockwise, the knives are serrated on the correct side for left-handed slicing, and the measuring cups have gradations printed on both sides. If you have a left handed friend, you might want to give him a left-handed aboriginal boomerang from Australia. Something you don't see everywhere!

Illustrated catalog 50¢

# LEKVAR BY THE BARREL
## H. ROTH & SON
**Uptown: 1577 First Ave.**
**New York, N.Y. 10028**
**Downtown: 968 Second Ave.**
**New York, N.Y. 10022**

PRODUCTS:

boards, cutting
boards, noodle
bottle cappers
bowls, mixing, copper
butter curlers
cake decorating sets
casseroles
casseroles, copper
cauldrons
clam steamers
cleavers
coffee makers
coffee makers, Turkish
coffee roasters
colanders, copper
cookie/noodle makers
corks/crowns/caps
corkscrews
couscous cookers
cups, measuring
cups, measuring, copper
cutters, biscuit
cutters, cole slaw
cutters, cookie
cutters, noodle
cutters, pineapple
cutters, ravioli
cutters, vegetable
dough kneaders
dripping jars

fermentation locks
flan rings
forks, fondue
French cruller bag sets
grinders, cheese
grinders, coffee
grinders, meat, electric
grinders, meat, manual
grinders, nut
grinders, salt/pepper
grinders, spice
icing syringes
irons, timbale
juicers
knives, carbon steel
krimp cut sealers
ladles
larding needles
mincers
molds, butter
molds, cake
molds, candy
molds, chocolate
molds, copper
molds, gelatine
molds, ice cream
molds, tart
mortars & pestles, brass
mortars & pestles, wood
pans, asparagus boiler

# LEKVAR BY THE BARREL (Cont'd)

pans, au gratin
pans, au gratin, enamel
pans, baking, enamel
pans, bread
pans, cake, springform
pans, crepe suzette, enamel
pans, double boiler
pans, double boiler, copper
pans, eclair
pans, enameled cast iron
pans, fish boiler
pans, fondue, copper
pans, fry, copper
pans, fry, steel
pans, omelet
pans, sauce, copper
pans, strudel
pitters, cherry
popcorn poppers
potato mashers
presses, butter
presses, cookie
presses, garlic
ricers
rollers, springerle cookie
rolling pins
salad baskets
sausage stuffers
scales
shrimp shellers
skewers
slicers
slicers, bean
slicers, meat
snail dishes
snail dough makers
souffle dishes
spaetzle machines
spatulas, stainless steel
spigots, wood
spoons, mixing
springerle boards
stands, cake
steak hammers
steam baskets
steam pudding forms
strainers, fruit/vegetable
strainers, tea
thermometers, alcohol
tubes, cake decorating
tubes, cannoli
tubes, cream roll
tubes, pastry
utensil sets, copper
utensil sets, wood
waffle irons, top of stove
water kettles, copper
whips
whisks
wine making kits
woks, steel

The products listed above are only an indication of what you'll find in Lekvar by the Barrel's catalog. For instance, they offer five different models of spaetzle machines. Spaetzles are small dumplings used by continental chefs as a potato substitute. In the scales department they have six models

# LEKVAR BY THE BARREL (Cont'd)

available. In the cookie cutter category they have everything you've ever heard of plus lots of things you've never seen. One section of their catalog is called "L'Utensils de Cafe du Paree." There they have Madeleine plaques (pans for making traditional French teacakes), flan rings, batteau molds, timbale molds for Baba au rhum, Charlotte molds and an English tart pan. They have two pages of coffee makers. If you're looking for enameled cast iron cookware, they have an extensive selection, including Doufeu self-basting ovens (like Dutch ovens) and chicken fry pans with lids. For those of you who collect copperware, they have a beautiful selection, including miniatures. They claim to carry everything for cooking or baking. They may be right.

Illustrated catalog free


## LEWIS & CONGER
39-25 Skilman Ave.
Long Island City, N.Y. 11104

PRODUCTS:

bacon cookers
boards, carving
boards, cutting
bottles, carbonater
casseroles, ceramic
cheese making kits
clam/oyster openers
coffee makers
coffee makers, cappuccino
colanders
cream makers
dough kneaders
egg scissors
grills, top of stove

grinders, cheese
grinders, salt/pepper
grinders, universal
hibachis, cast iron
ice cream freezers, refrigerator
immersion heaters
jar openers
juicers
knives, stainless steel
lasagne dishes
mincers
pans, asparagus boiler
pans, omelet
pans, sauce

## LEWIS & CONGER (Cont'd)

roasting pins
roasting racks
scales
shears
skillets, partitioned
slicers
slicers, bean

smokers, electric
spoons, mustache
steam baskets
strainers, vegetable/fruit
water filters
water purifiers
yogurt making equipment

This company has all kinds of things to order by mail, including bicycles, radios, tableware, bar accessories and kitchen utensils. Among the items offered are an "eggs-ray," a little battery-operated machine for checking the freshness of eggs, and an electric smoker for smoking your own poultry, fish, game and fowl. A lot of the things in their catalog are unnecessary gadgets, but may be what you've been looking for anyway. Generally interesting and unusual.

Illustrated catalog free

## LIBERTY ORGANIZATION
P.O. Box 306
Montrose, Calif. 91020

PRODUCTS:

knife sharpeners, butcher's steel
knives, carbon steel
knives, rustproof steel

This company distributes the famous knives of the Dick Company, kitchen and butcher knives that most of the professional people are using. Soon they will add the Forschner-Victorinox line of Swiss cutlery. They have paring knives, cook's knives, bread slicers, ham slicers and boning knives. Also available are several models of steels for sharpening, including

## LIBERTY ORGANIZATION (Cont'd)

a pocket-sized steel. You may also order magnetic bars to mount on the wall for holding your knives. This saves on cut fingers—no sharp edges hiding in a drawer.

Illustrated brochure free

## LILLIAN VERNON CORP.
510 South Fulton Ave.
Mount Vernon, N.Y. 10550

PRODUCTS:

| | |
|---|---|
| boards, cutting | pans, broiler |
| bowls, mixing, copper | pans, omelet |
| colanders | roast holders |
| corkscrews | shish kebab sets |
| covers & lids, fry, see-thru | slicers/shredders |
| cups, measuring | souffle dishes |
| dripping jars | spice racks, wood |
| egg coddlers | spoons, mixing |
| forks, giant | sprouters, animal-shaped |
| funnels | steam racks |
| grinders, salt/pepper | tea infusers |
| ice cream freezers, manual | tongs |
| mortars & pestles, ceramic | utensil sets, wood |
| mortars & pestles, wood | whisks |
| oven spades | woks, stainless steel |

Gifts and goodies from seashells to silver polish, as well as utensils. Lots of handy things for the kitchen, such as a brush to clean your can opener, mortar and pestle sets for crushing your herbs, and a fold-over omelet pan for the perfect omelet. Unusual items like egg coddlers. (Just put in an egg (without the shell) with seasonings, simmer it gently in water, remove the chrome-plated top, and Presto! a tasty egg

# LILLIAN VERNON CORP. (Cont'd)

in a beautiful porcelain server.) Many more useful items in their enticing catalog. Good quality and good prices.

96 page color illustrated catalog free to customers

# LODGE MANUFACTURING CO.
6th St. at Railroad Ave.
Box 380
South Pittsburg, Tenn. 37380

PRODUCTS:

| | |
|---|---|
| Dutch ovens, cast iron | pans, fry, cast iron |
| griddles, cast iron | pans, muffin, cast iron |
| hibachis, cast iron | pans, sauce, cast iron |
| pans, bread, cast iron | skillets, cast iron |

A complete line of cast iron cookware, including a variety of bread pans, pop-over pans, muffin pans, lamb forms, bundt pans, corn stick pans, bread stick pans, French loaf pans, etc. Cast iron is a very desirable metal for cookware. Not only does it maintain the heat, but it distributes it evenly. It is one of the few products that can claim, "The older it is, the better it is."

Color illustrated brochure free

**MAGIC MILL**
235 West Second South
Salt Lake City, Utah 84101

PRODUCTS:

    dough kneaders
    grinders, grain, stone
    mixers, electric

The Magic Mill is a handsomely designed home food grinder. It features a grinding adjustment with which you can vary the grind between cereal (coarse) and pastry flour (fine). The unit is basically electric, but comes with a manual conversion handle. The cabinet is available in walnut or polished maple, and the design is one of simple elegance. The Magic Mixer is a combination dough mixer/kneader and blender. Up to five loaves of bread may be kneaded at one time. There are optional attachments for juicing, cutting and shredding, mincing, squeezing lemons, and making ice cream. The Magic Mill comes with a two year guarantee against defects in workmanship and materials, the Magic Mixer with a one year guarantee.

Illustrated brochure free

**MAID OF SCANDINAVIA COMPANY**
3244 Raleigh Ave.
Minneapolis, Minn. 55416

PRODUCTS:

beaters
boards, cake
boards, cutting
bottle cappers
bottles, carbonater
bowls, mixing, copper
bowls, mixing, stainless steel
cake decorating sets
cake dividers
cake ornaments
cheese making kits
colanders

## MAID OF SCANDINAVIA (Cont'd)

cookie irons
cookie/noodle makers
cookie sheets
cups, measuring
cutters, bearclaw
cutters, biscuit
cutters, cake
cutters, cole slaw
cutters, cookie
cutters, corn kernel
cutters, noodle
cutters, noodle, blades
cutters, pineapple
cutters, tart
dough kneaders
egg poachers
flan rings
forks, meat (giant)
funnels
griddles, electric
griddles, top of stove
grinders, cheese
grinders, chocolate
grinders, coffee, manual
grinders, nut
grinders, salt/pepper
ice cream freezers, electric
icing syringes
irons, timbale
knife sharpeners
knives, cake
krimp cut sealers
ladles
lemon wedge squeezers
mincers
molds, cake
molds, candy
molds, cookie
molds, gelatine
molds, ice cream
molds, tart
mortars & pestles, wood
noodle making machines
oven spades
pans, baking, stainless steel
pans, bread
pans, broiler
pans, cake
pans, cake, springform
pans, double boiler
pans, eclair
pans, fondue
pans, muffin
pans, omelet
pans, pie
pans, pizza
peelers
pie jaggers
presses, burger
presses, cookie
presses, garlic
roasting racks
rollers, docker
rollers, pastry
sausage making kits
sausage stuffers
scales
scoops, aluminum
scoops, ice cream
scoops, wooden
skewers
skillets, partitioned
slicers
slicers, cake

## MAID OF SCANDINAVIA (Cont'd)

slicers, cheese
slicers, meat
souffle dishes
spatulas
spatulas, stainless steel
spoons, measuring
spoons, mixing
Springerle boards
stands, cake
steam pudding forms
strainers, fruit/vegetable
thermometer forks
thermometers
thermometers, candy
thermometers, dough
thermometers, meat
timers
tongs
tubes, cake decorating
tubes, cannoli
tubes, cream roll
tubes, pastry
utensil sets, melamine
utensil sets, nylon
utensil sets, wood
waffle irons, Scandinavian
waffle irons, top of stove
whippers, charger
whips
whisks
wine making kits
woks, steel

yogurt making equipment

Whew! Where to start in telling you about Maid of Scandinavia? They are a mail-order company dealing in unusual baking equipment and cake decorating materials. It would be hard to imagine anything along those lines that they don't have. Their cake pans come in every conceivable shape and variety of size. You want a square angel food pan? They have it. Extra deep pans, a half dozen or so models of Bundt pans, including Bundt style muffin pans, many shapes in tiered sets, Charlotte molds, full bell cake molds, and on and on. They also have hundreds of shapes of molds for making candy, lollipops and frozen suckers. For decorating your cakes they have all kinds of ornaments and icing decorations, and to serve them beautifully, doillies, including gold and silver ones, cake boards and the most incredible cake stands. They also specialize in gifts and party favors. A vast line of items for the bride and wedding attendants, special things for baby showers, holidays, and parties to celebrate sports events. If

## MAID OF SCANDINAVIA (Cont'd)

you're planning a "big to do" for Christmas, a family gathering, or just giving a party, you'll find lots of inspiration in their catalogs.

Illustrated catalogs $1.00

## MANGANARO'S FOOD, INC.
488 Ninth Ave.
New York, N.Y. 10018

PRODUCTS:

| | |
|---|---|
| coffee makers, espresso | grinders, salt/pepper |
| corkscrews | irons, pizzelle |
| cutters, noodle | noodle making machines |
| cutters, ravioli | presses, garlic |
| forks, snail | rollers, ravioli |
| funnels, sausage | strainers, tomato |
| grinders, cheese | tongs |
| grinders, coffee, manual | tongs, snail |
| tubes, cannoli | |

Italian gourmet foods and utensils for serving and preparing them are the items you can mail order from Manganaro's. Three models of espresso makers are offered; a gnocchi and cavatelle machine, a noodle making machine with eight different noodle thicknesses possible. Looking through their exotic catalog is a gustatory trip to the old world. Don't read it when you're hungry—you'll starve to death.

Catalog free

## MEADOWS MILL CO.
P.O. Box 1288
North Wilkesboro, N.C. 28659

PRODUCTS:

grinders, grain, stone

Manufacturers of the Meadows 8" Household Stone Burr Mill, a grain grinding mill fitted with two genuine native granite stones. This unit is designed to grind all types of dry, free-flowing grains up to and including large corn grains. Also available are various larger mills for commercial use, including a 1000 pound, all steel grits separator, presumably to be used by establishments catering to large numbers of southerners.

Illustrated brochure free

## MILES KIMBALL
295 Bond St.
Oshkosh, Wisc. 54901

PRODUCTS:

bakers, top of stove
boards, cutting
colanders
corks
covers & lids, fry, see-thru
cutters, corn kernel
egg poachers
forks, meat (giant)
grinders, cheese
jar openers
juicers
pans, blanching/canning
pans, broiler
pans, cake
pans, roasting
pans, sauce
peelers
presses, garlic
skillets, partitioned
slicers/shredders
spatulas, stainless steel
sprouters
strainers, fruit/vegetable
tea infusers
tongs
tongs, salad
woks

## MILES KIMBALL (Cont'd)

Kitchenwares are only a small part of what this mail-order company has to offer. They also have door mats, chandelier spray, beach towels and golf balls—among other things. Lots of things that aren't listed in our product list are useful in the kitchen, though, like automatic coffeepot starters and many accessories for the home freezer. They go for plastics and teflon and disposable items in a big way.

Color illustrated catalog free

## NATURAL TECHNOLOGY DESIGN
Wolcott, Vt. 05680

PRODUCTS:

grinder/press combos

This company makes several models of a complete home fruit grinder/cider press ranging in price from $65.00 to $250.00, depending on size and electric-hydraulic options. Whether you're an individual suburban dweller, countryman or part of a school or community group wanting to make your own cider or wine, one of these machines is what you'll need to do the job.

Brochure free

**PETER NILES
   OUTDOORSMAN AND
   INTERNATIONAL
   SHOPPER**
911 Walker
Houston, Tex. 77002

PRODUCTS:

coffee makers

The Incafe Coffee Carafe brews a pure coffee concentrate with cold water. Hot water is then added to the concentrate, producing coffee without the acidity, oiliness and bitterness that are by-products of hot water brewing. This method of coffee making is said to have been invented by the ancient Incas.

Illustrated brochure free

**NORDIC STOVE SHOPPE
   —VIKING HOMESTEAD**
34 Pearl St., Box 268
Dover, N.H. 03820

PRODUCTS:

stoves, coal/wood

Jøtul 100% cast iron stoves and fireplaces from Norway. You can cook on top of any flat-topped stove, of which they have several models. They also offer a kitchen stove with two range-top hotplates, oven with enameled baking sheet and solid pressed steel enameled roasting tin, adjusting damper for cooking and baking. This particular stove is finished in black fireproof enamel for easy cleaning. Several stove models come with enamel finish and traditional relief cast designs of lions, moose, etc., to fancy up your homestead. They claim

## NORDIC STOVE SHOPPE (Cont'd)

to work better than an Ashley—so if you're paying for your firewood, take heed.

Illustrated brochure free

## NORTHWESTERN COFFEE MILLS
217 N. Broadway
Milwaukee, Wisc. 53202

PRODUCTS:

| | |
|---|---|
| coffee makers | grinders, coffee, electric |
| coffee makers, espresso | grinders, coffee, manual |
| coffee makers, Turkish | tea infusers |

This company sells oriental teas, coffees, herb teas, spices and wild rice in addition to their grinders and coffee makers. They have four varieties of drip grind coffee maker as well as Turkish and espresso types. Also a filter-type tea brewer.

Illustrated catalog free

## PAPRIKAS WEISS IMPORTER
1546 Second Ave.
New York, N.Y. 10028

PRODUCTS:

| | |
|---|---|
| apple corers | coffee makers, Turkish |
| basters, pyrex | colanders |
| boards, bread | corkscrews |
| boards, noodle | couscous cookers |
| bowls, mixing, copper | cups, measuring |
| bowls, mixing, stainless steel | cups, measuring, glass |
| butter curlers | cutters, biscuit |
| casseroles, copper | cutters, cookie |
| coffee makers | cutters, noodle |
| coffee makers, espresso | cutters, pastry |

## PAPRIKAS WEISS IMPORTER (Cont'd)

cutters, ravioli
dough kneaders
Dutch ovens, cast iron
egg poachers
egg separators
flan rings
friers, deep fat, electric
griddles, top of stove
grills, electric
grinders, cheese
grinders, coffee
grinders, meat
grinders, salt/pepper
grinders, spice
ice cream freezers, electric
juice extractors
knives, carbon steel
knives, clam/oyster
krimp cut sealers
larding needles
lemon wedge squeezers
mincers
molds, aluminum
molds, butter
molds, cake
molds, pate
pans, cake
pans, crepe suzette
pans, double boiler
pans, ebleskiver
pans, eclair
pans, fish boiler
pans, fondue, copper
pans, fry, aluminum
pans, fry, cast iron
pans, fry, copper
pans, muffin, cast iron
pans, omelet
pans, sauce, aluminum
pans, sauce, cast iron
pans, sauce, copper
pastry brushes
pitters, cherry
presses, duck
presses, fruit
presses, garlic
presses, onion
ricers
rollers, springerle cookie
rolling pins
sausage stuffers
shears, poultry
shrimp shellers
skimmers
slicers
slicers, bean
slicers/shredders
souffle dishes
spatulas, stainless steel
spatulas, wood
spoons, long
spoons, mixing
steak hammers
steam baskets
steam pudding forms
stock pots
strainers, tea
strainers, tomato
tea infusers
toasters, sandwich
tubes, cannoli
waffle irons, Scandinavian

## PAPRIKAS WEISS IMPORTER (Cont'd)

Food is this company's first and main concern, and the extensive list of their kitchenware should give an idea of the scope of their operation. The Weiss family began to sell Hungarian spices to their fellow immigrants over fifty years ago. Today the business is one of the largest importers of gourmet delicacies and gourmet cookware from all over the world. The store, as reflected in their delightful catalog, still maintains the authentic "folksy" old world atmosphere with which it began. Spices and herbs are displayed in open bins, much as in a turn of the century marketplace. The cookware available is high quality, diverse and novel. Available, for instance, is a sandwich toaster—a double-handled device for toasting any manner of sandwich over an open fire. If you want culinary inspiration and armchair travel, browse through their catalog.

63 page illustrated catalog free

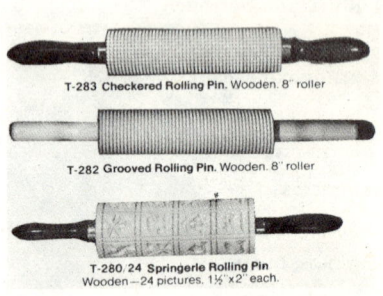

## PFEIL & HOLING, INC.
5 White St.
New York, N.Y. 10013

PRODUCTS:

| | |
|---|---|
| boards, cake | molds, gelatine |
| bowls, mixing, stainless steel | molds, ice cream |
| cake decorating sets | molds, tart |
| cake ornaments | oven spades |
| cookie sheets | pans, bread |
| cutters, cake | pans, cake |
| cutters, cookie | pans, cake, springform |
| dough dividers, expansion | pans, muffin |
| icing syringes | pans, pie |
| knives, stainless steel | pie jaggers |
| molds, cake | pitters, plum |
| molds, chocolate | rollers, docker |

## PFEIL & HOLING, INC. (Cont'd)

rollers, pastry
rollers, springerle cookie
rolling pins
scales
scoops, aluminum
scoops, ice cream
scoops, plastic

slicers, cake
spatulas, stainless steel
spoons, measuring
spoons, mixing
stands, cake
tongs
tubes, cake decorating

whips

Kitchen and cooking utensils with an emphasis on baking and cake decorating. A very complete line of ornaments for special occasions like weddings and children's parties in both plastic and sugar. They have an extensive variety of shaped cake pans and molds for making hearts, rings, cloverleafs, Santas, rabbits, stars, zodiacs, etc. Cookie cutters come in hundreds of shapes, too. They also have a line of professional bakery machinery, including mixers and grating/slicing machines, all heavy duty. And, if you're really into cake decorating, they also have airbrush guns and compressors.

Complete set of catalogs $1.00

## PORTLAND STOVE FOUNDRY CO.
57 Kennebec St.
Portland, Me. 04104

PRODUCTS:

casseroles, cast iron
Dutch ovens, cast iron
grills, fireplace

pans, fry, cast iron
pans, muffin, cast iron
pans, sauce, cast iron

stoves, coal/wood

This New England foundry has been producing high quality cast iron products since 1877. Their molds are made by hand, and their designs are classic and beautiful. Many of their cast iron ranges are adaptable for wood, coal or oil. The Queen

# PORTLAND STOVE FOUNDRY CO. (Cont'd)

Atlantic Range is a design that dates back to the beginnings of American history. This company is still turning them out, and—given the durability of cast iron ranges—they will continue to be seen for a long time to come. These ranges are available in porcelain enamel finish, as well as plain cast iron. The Portland Stove Foundry Company also offers a line of cookware made of cast iron and finished in enamel. This is called Cloverleaf Ware, and items are being added all the time to the line. If you have a feeling for early American beauty of design in cast iron stoves and cookware, you will like what this company has to offer.

Illustrated brochure free

# PRESQUE ISLAND WINE CELLARS
9449 Buffalo Road
North East, Penn. 16428

« MILANO » Crushing stemmering machine

CrSt  425.00
(Shipped via truck, freight collect.)
(see note)

PRODUCTS:

acid testing kits, wine
barrels
bottle brushes
bottle cappers
bottle corkers
bottle fillers
bottles, wine
bungs, wood
carboy/bottle rinsers
carboys, wine
cork extracters
corks/crowns/caps, wine
corkscrews
crushers/stemmers
crushers, fruit
ebulliometers

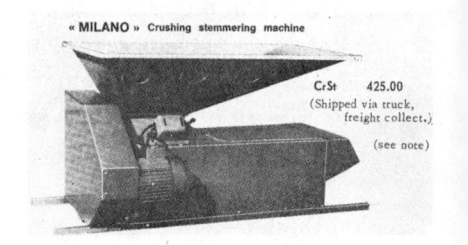

fermentation locks
funnels
hydrometer jars
hydrometers
pinchcocks
presses, fruit
scales
siphons
stoppers, rubber
sugar testing kits, wine
thermometers
vinometers
wine filters
winemaking kits
wine thieves

## PRESQUE ISLAND WINE CELLARS (Cont'd)

For the home winemaker this company offers everything you need, including books, chemicals, grape concentrates and utensils. Their catalog is full of helpful hints and good advice to put you on the right track. Instructions come with all the items you may not be familiar with. If you still can't come up with a vino that suits you, then you may order from a wide variety of table wines from their own cellars.

Catalog free

**R & R MILL CO.**
45 West First North
Smithfield, Utah 84335

PRODUCTS:

| | |
|---|---|
| bottle cappers | grinders, universal |
| can sealers | ice cream freezers |
| canning jar lifters | juicers |
| churns, electric | pitters, cherry |
| cutters, corn kernel | presses, fruit/vegetable |
| donut makers | pressure cookers |
| dough kneaders | ricers |
| Dutch ovens, cast iron | sausage stuffers |
| griddles, cast iron | skillets, cast iron |
| grinders, cheese | slicers |
| grinders, coffee, manual | slicers, bean |
| grinders, electric | slicers/shredders |
| grinders, grain | steam baskets |
| grinders, grain, stone | stoves, coal/wood |
| grinders, meat, electric | strainers, fruit/vegetable |
| grinders, rotary | water distillers |
| | water kettles, copper |

This company's line of utensils is especially important to the homemaker who does canning and food preparation from the garden or farm. If you grind your own flour or make your

### R & R MILL CO. (Cont'd)

own butter or have an orchard of fruit to process, you'll want to look through their catalog for things to help your work. They have a great variety of grinding mills to offer, ranging from $10.95 to $195.00. You can grind grains for cereal or flour, salt, coffee, shells, roots, bark, nuts, seeds, etc. Also available are several models of dough kneaders. If you belong to an organization that likes to raise money with bake sales, or if you're just trying to break the tie with rising supermarket prices, this kind of equipment is a good investment.

Illustrated catalog free


### RADIANT GRATE, INC.
31 Morgan Park
Clinton, Conn. 06413

PRODUCTS:

fireplace grates
fireplace ovens
fireplace rotisseries
fireplace stoves
grills, fireplace
hearth reflectors

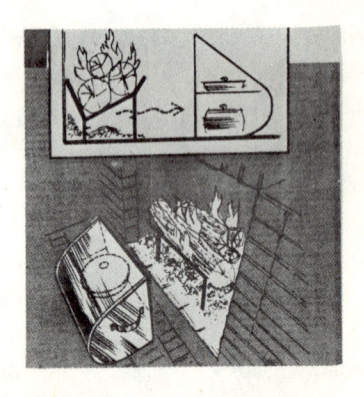

The Radiant Grate is a patented invention of Mr. Emil Dahlquist. Basically, it is a normal fireplace grate with the front edge elevated, thus forming a pocket under the coals which traps the heat and radiates it outward across the hearth. In times of fuel crisis and energy shortage, this is an excellent way to maximize the efficiency of your fireplace. Moreover, the concentration of heat over the hearth provides a clean and economical way of cooking. This possibility has been further developed by Mr. Dahlquist in his stove, oven, rotisserie and grill—all designed for use in combination with the Radiant Grate. Aside from the obvious economic benefits of

## RADIANT GRATE CO. (Cont'd)

fireplace cooking, it is possible to cook many things in less time than on a conventional stove. Mr. Dahlquist claims that a four pound roast may be well done in one hour, and that a one inch steak is cooked in one minute. Because the cooking is done in front of the fireplace, there are no smoke-blackened utensils to deal with, nor does greasy smoke escape into the flue. The Radiant Grate is an example of yankee ingenuity and the ancient art of hearth cooking combined with a new wrinkle.

Illustrated brochure free

RETSEL INC.
P.O. Box 291
McCammon, Idaho

**CORONA STONE MILL BY RETSEL**

Now a hand mill with Stones! Identical to the Corona, except it has stones. You can grind fine flour in one operation. No heating problems. The perfect grinder to keep with your wheat storage. You don't need to depend on any outside power to grind flour. Easily adjusted to coarse or fine grind. The stones are made to last for years and will not need dressing. The stones are manufactured especially for the Corona hand mill and are bound with a special bonding that will allow no flaking off. Easily assembled and easy to use.

PRODUCTS:

dough kneaders
grinder/blender combos
grinders, baby food
grinders, electric
grinders, grain, stone
meat saws
mixers, electric
pressure cookers
sprouters, plastic
stoves, camp
stoves, coal/wood
water kettles

This company specializes in equipment for the self-sufficient homestead. They sell canning-size pressure cookers, spinning wheels, Aladdin lamps, saws, drying and storage units, including a fiberglass root cellar. Several models of grain grinders are offered, one of which can be converted from manual to electric when you finally get your power in. Back to the land people will find much in this catalog to interest them, especially an article on what foods and dry goods to store, how to store them, and how long they'll keep fresh.

Illustrated catalog free

**ROSENTHAL STUDIO-HAUS**
584 Fifth Ave.
New York, N.Y. 10036

PRODUCTS:

boards, carving
boards, cutting
casseroles, enamel
coffee makers
forks, meat (giant)
forks, salad serving
grinders, salt/pepper
knives, stainless steel
ladles
pans, fondue, cast iron
pans, fry, enamel
pans, sauce, enamel
souffle dishes
utensil sets

This company brings together the world of art and the necessities of living. Their basic product, as they see it, is the mood or atmosphere of the dining table. They employ artists and designers of original and daring vision, and each of their designs is submitted—before production begins—to an independent committee of designers and art critics for evaluation. Recently they have become interested in cookware, and while the emphasis is still on the table, their lines of cutlery, ceramic cookware and wooden kitchen utensils reflect the high standards of beauty and originality already established. The catalog and various brochures available cost nothing, and are works of art in themselves.

20 page color illustrated catalog and various brochures free

**SALTWATER FARM**
Varrell Lane
York Harbor, Me. 03911

PRODUCTS:

clam steamers
shears

This company specializes in shipping live Maine lobsters; also clams, salmon and other assorted seafood delicacies. Among

## SALTWATER FARM (Cont'd)

the items you'll need to take advantage of their goodies, besides a hefty bank account, are shears to cut up your lobster and clam steamers to cook your clams. You can order all except the bank account from them.

Color illustrated catalog free

**SEMPLEX OF U.S.A.**
4805 Lyndale Ave. No.
Minneapolis, Minn. 55412

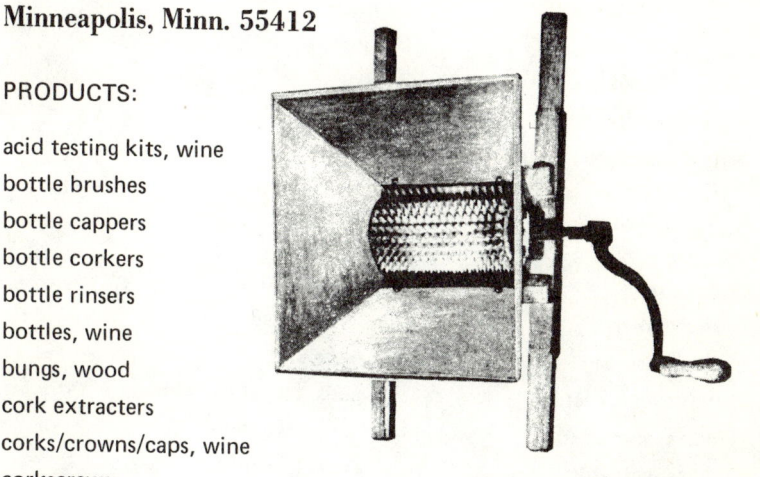

PRODUCTS:

acid testing kits, wine
bottle brushes
bottle cappers
bottle corkers
bottle rinsers
bottles, wine
bungs, wood
cork extracters
corks/crowns/caps, wine
corkscrews
crushers, fruit
fermentation containers, plastic
fermentation locks
funnels
hydrometers
presses, fruit
spigots, wood
spoons, long
stoppers, plastic
stoppers, rubber
sulphur locks
thermometers

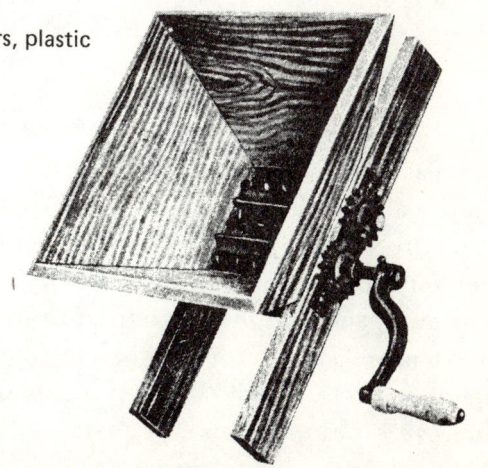

## SEMPLEX OF U.S.A. (Cont'd)

vinometers
wine filters
wine thieves
yogurt making kits

Many ingredients and recipes for making your own wine and beer, and the equipment to do it with. Several models of crushers and presses are offered that are suitable for the amateur winemaker. Prompt shipment of mail orders.

Catalog free

## THE SMILIE COMPANY
575 Howard St.
San Francisco, Calif. 94105

PRODUCTS:

boilers, large
coffee makers
cups, measuring
Dutch ovens, cast iron
griddles, aluminum
griddles, cast iron
grills, fireplace
ladles
lifters, aluminum
lifters, steel
mess kits
pans, fry, aluminum
pans, fry, steel
pans, fry, teflon
pans, nesting
spatulas, nylon
stoves, camp

Offered is a complete assortment of gear for outdoor living. Thermal underwear? Swiss Army knives? Snakebite kits? They're all here, along with high quality sleeping bags, tents, air mattresses, and just about anything else that you might need for camping—be it in the Snake River wilderness or your own back yard. An attractive feature of the catalog is an extensive list of outdoor books, including books on mountaineering, woodlore, camp cookbooks, and area guidebooks.

63 page illustrated catalog 10¢

**SUNSET HOUSE**
219 Sunset Building
Beverly Hills, Calif. 90215

PRODUCTS:

| | |
|---|---|
| bakers, top of stove | immersion heaters |
| boards, cutting | irons, timbale |
| corks | juicers |
| cups, custard | knives, vanadium steel |
| donut makers | pans, broiler |
| egg cookers | pans, cake |
| egg poachers | salad baskets |
| forks, meat (giant) | skillets, partitioned |
| griddles, top of stove | slicers |
| grills, top of stove | sprouters, animal-shaped |
| ice cream freezers, manual | steam racks |

utensil sets, wood

Gadgets galore! Any useful little thing you can think of is in this catalog. In the sprouter category, they have one shaped like a man's head, one shaped like a ram, and a nice hanging bowl-shaped one. Chia seeds grow on them, which look interesting and are a very nutritious addition to your salads. Most things from this company have an extra twist of some sort. Their cutting board is designed so that you can cut on the block end and slide foods into the tray end, eliminating the problem of what to put it in till you assemble your salad or whatever. Other interesting things to order from their catalog are light bulbs that burn for ten years and ginseng, aloe vera and banana plants.

Color illustrated catalog free

**VERMONT SOAPSTONE CO., INC.**
Perkinsville, Vt. 05151

PRODUCTS:

griddles, soapstone

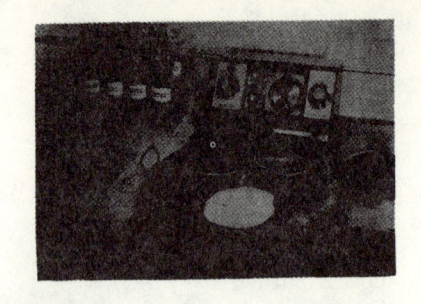

This is a one-family operation producing soapstone products such as boot driers, ashtrays and bread basket warmers. The soapstone is processed completely on the premises—from its natural state to the finely crafted products that are sold. Soapstone is a soft, fine-grained stone that is easily carved, beautiful and durable. Soapstone griddles produce greaseless pancakes, since no grease is needed, and can be restored to the original finish with a light sanding.

Illustrated brochure free

**WALNUT ACRES**
Penns Creek, Penn. 17862

PRODUCTS:

grinders, baby food
grinders, cheese
grinders, grain
pans, bread
pans, broiler
scales
slicers, cheese
sprouters
steam baskets
water filters
water purifiers
yogurt making equipment

This is a good company to know about if you're doing quantity buying. They ship grains, flours, teas, vitamins and pasta

## WALNUT ACRES (Cont'd)

products as well as many prepared foods. Their prices are reasonable and they are a very professional mail order house. They grow most of the products they sell and do their own freezing and canning. Generally strict about labeling and letting you know what's organic and unsprayed. Their line of kitchen items is useful and economical. They seem to be concerned for your health and your pocketbook.

Catalog free

**WESTON BOWL MILL**
Main St.
Weston, Vt. 05161

PRODUCTS:

| | |
|---|---|
| boards, bread | ladles |
| boards, carving | molds, butter |
| boards, cheese | mortars & pestles, wood |
| boards, cutting | nutcrackers |
| bowls, mixing, wooden | potato mashers |
| cleavers | rollers, springerle cookie |
| corkscrews | rolling pins |
| forks, salad serving | scoops, wooden |
| grinders, salt/pepper | slicers |
| knife sharpeners | slicers/shredders |
| knife sharpeners, butcher's steel | spoons, mixing |
| knives, carbon steel | steak hammers |

tongs, salad

This mill makes all sorts of wooden items for the home from maple, yellow, grey and white birch, French cherrywood, Vermont pine and oak. They have some beautiful children's toys as well as furniture, clocks and birdfeeders. Their mixing and serving bowls come in all sizes and their cutting boards also have a great variety of size and shape. They offer Lazy Susans, knife holders, spoon racks, egg cups, napkin rings—

## WESTON BOWL MILL (Cont'd)

in fact, a vast array of kitchenwares made from wood. Wooden utensils and other kitchenware, if well cared for, seem to add a sense of warmth and harmony to food preparation that no other material can match. If you too like the feel of using wooden items, then you'll be very satisfied with this company. In these days of throwaway, garish plastics, it's somehow a comfort just to look at this catalog.

47 page illustrated catalog 25¢

## WHITE MOUNTAIN FREEZER, INC.
Lincoln Ave. Ext., Box 231
Winchendon, Mass. 01475

PRODUCTS:

ice cream freezers, electric
ice cream freezers, manual

Freezers in a range of sizes from two quarts to 20 quarts. All cast iron parts with tubs of New England pine or high density polyethylene foam plastic. Homemade ice cream is certainly one of the joys of life, and here's what you need to make it. Ingredients to make your own ice cream are readily available, and it's fun and easy to do.

Color illustrated brochure free

**WILTON ENTERPRISES, INC.**
833 West 115th St.
Chicago, Ill. 60643

PRODUCTS:

boards, cake
cake decorating sets
cake dividers
cake ornaments
cookie sheets
cutters, cookie
molds, cake
molds, candy
molds, chocolate
molds, gelatine

funnels
knives, cake
molds, ice cream
molds, sugar
pans, muffin
presses, cookie
spatulas
stands, cake
tubes, cake decorating

Wilton's is definitely "the" cake decorating company. By all means order their elegant and witty catalog and take a look at expert cake decorating. Their catalog offers valuable and easy to understand instructions on how to achieve the most beautiful effects. The latest catalog shows a Cinderella cake and castle mold that is a fairytale come true. Their line of cake ornaments is marvelous. Wilton's is guaranteed to inspire you to take up cake decorating even if you've never set foot in a kitchen before.

Color illustrated catalog $1.50

**WINECRAFT**
Box 94
Northboro, Mass. 01532

PRODUCTS:

corking machines
corks/crowns/caps, wine
fermentation locks

hydrometers
wine filters
winemaking kits

## WINECRAFT (Cont'd)

Besides the hardware necessary for winemaking, this company sells yeasts, acids, tannin, stabilizers, etc. The owners are home winemakers and have tested all the products they sell. They include recipes and tips for the beginner in their kits.

Catalog free

## WISCONSIN CHEESE MAKERS GUILD
**6048 West Beloit Road
Milwaukee, Wisc. 53219**

PRODUCTS:

bean pots, electric
boards, cheese
boards, cutting
coffee makers
egg cookers
grinders, salt/pepper
hot dog cookers
pans, broiler
pans, fondue, electric
pans, omelet
popcorn poppers
toaster/broilers

This company has gift packages of a variety of Wisconsin cheese and all-beef summer sausage, many of them packaged along with the utensils listed above. For instance, the electric fondue pot and forks comes with two packages of ready-to-heat and eat Swiss fondue and chocolate fondue for dessert, plus a recipe book. The omelet pan comes with a variety of cheese and preserves and recipes. Probably not the cheapest way to buy an omelet pan, but maybe the most fun.

Illustrated catalog free

# MASTER INDEX

ACID testing kits, wine
   Presque Isle Wine Cellars
   Semplex of U.S.A.
ALCOHOL thermometer, (see
      Thermometers, alcohol)
APPLE corers
   Cross Imports, Inc.
   Paprikas Weiss Importer
APPLE peelers, (see Peelers,
   apple)
ASPARAGUS pans, (see Pans,
   asparagus)
AU GRATIN pans, (see Pans, au
   gratin)
BABA rhum cups, (see Cups, baba
   rhum)
BABY food grinders, (see Grinders,
   baby food)
BACON cookers
   Lewis & Conger
BAKERS, top of stove
   Fashionable
   Miles Kimball
   Sunset House
BAKING pans, (see Pans, Baking)
BAR units, automatic
   Bissinger's
BARRELS
   Presque Isle Wine Cellars

BASKETS, salad, (see Salad baskets)
BASKETS, steam, (see Steam baskets)
BASTERS, aluminum
   Bazaar de la Cuisine
BASTERS, nylon
   Cross Imports, Inc.
BASTERS, pyrex
   Paprikas Weiss Importer
BASTERS, stainless steel
   Bazaar de la Cuisine
   Fashionable
BEAN pots
   The Blue Owl
BEAN pots, electric
   Wisconsin Cheese Makers Guild
BEAN slicers, (see Slicers, bean)
BEAR claw cutters, (see Cutters,
   bear claw)
BEATERS
   Bazaar de la Cuisine
   Maid of Scandinavia Company
BISCUIT cutters, (see Cutters,
   biscuit)
BLANCHERS, (see Pans, blancher canning)
BLENDER combos, (see Grinder/
   blender combos)

BLENDERS, (see Juicers/blenders)
BOARDS, ( see Under specific type of board, i.e. bread board, cake board, carving board)
BOILERS, large
   The Smilie Company
BOTTLE brushes
   Presque Isle Wine Cellars
   Semplex of U.S.A.
BOTTLE cappers
   Homestead Industries
   Lekvar by the Barrel
   Maid of Scandinavia Company
   Presque Isle Wine Cellars
   R & R Mill Co.
   Semplex of U.S.A.
BOTTLE corkers
   Presque Isle Wine Cellars
   Semplex of U.S.A.
BOTTLE fillers
   Presque Isle Wine Cellars
BOTTLE rinsers
   Semplex of U.S.A.
BOTTLES, carbonater
   Lewis & Conger
   Maid of Scandinavia Company
BOTTLES, wine
   Presque Isle Wine Cellars
   Semplex of U.S.A.
BOWLS, mixing, ceramic
   Bennington Potters, Inc.
BOWLS, mixing, copper
   Bazaar de la Cuisine
   Lekvar by the Barrel
   Lillian Vernon Corp.
   Maid of Scandinavia Company
   Paprikas Weiss Importer
BOWLS, mixing, stainless steel
   Bazaar de la Cuisine
   Cross Imports, Inc.
   Fashionable
   Maid of Scandinavia Company
   Paprikas Weiss Importer
   Pfeil & Holing, Inc.
BOWLS, mixing, wooden
   Butcher Block & More
   Weston Bowl Mill
BREAD boards
   Bazaar de la Cuisine
   Paprikas Weiss Importer
   Weston Bowl Mill
BREAD knives, (see Knives, bread)
BREAD pans, (see Pans, bread)
BROILER racks
   Bazaar de la Cuisine
BROILER/rotisseries
   Braun North America
BROILERS, electric
   Cornwall Corporation
BROILERS, (see Ovens/broilers)
BROILER pans, (see Pans, broiler)
BROILERS/toasters, (see Toasters/broilers)
BRUSHES, bottle, (see Bottle brushes)
BRUSHES, pastry, (see Pastry brushes)
BUNGS, wood
   Presque Isle Wine Cellars
   Semplex of U.S.A.
BUTCHER block tables, (see also Carving boards)
   Butcher Block & More
   Forrest Jones, Inc.
BUTTER curlers
   Cross Imports, Inc.
   Hoffritz
   Lekvar by the Barrel
   Paprikas Weiss Importer
BUTTER molds, (see Molds, butter)
BUTTER presses, (see Presses, butter)
CAKE boards
   Cake Decorators
   Maid of Scandinavia Company
   Pfeil & Holing, Inc.
   Wilton Enterprises, Inc.
CAKE cutters, (see Cutters, cake)
CAKE decorating sets
   Bazaar de la Cuisine
   Cake Decorators
   Cross Imports, Inc.
   Lekvar by the Barrel
   Maid of Scandinavia Company
   Pfeil & Holing, Inc.
   Wilton Enterprises, Inc.
CAKE decorating tubes, (see Tubes, cake decorating)
CAKE dividers
   Cake Decorators
   Maid of Scandinavia Company
   Wilton Enterprises, Inc.
CAKE forks, (see Forks, cake)
CAKE knives, (see Knives, cake)
CAKE molds, (see Molds, cake)
CAKE ornaments
   Cake Decorators
   Maid of Scandinavia Company

Pfeil & Holing, Inc.
Wilton Enterprises, Inc.
CAKE pans, (see Pans, cake)
CAKE slicers, (see Slicers, cake)
CAKE stands, (see Stands, cake)
CAMP stoves, (see Stoves, camp)
CANDY molds, (see Molds, candy)
CANDY thermometers, (see Thermometers, candy)
CANNING pans (blancher), (see Pans, blancher-canning)
CANNOLI tubes, (see Tubes, cannoli)
CAN openers
  Cornwall Corporation
  Cross Imports, Inc.
  Hoffritz
CAN sealers
  R & R Mill Co.
CANNING jar lifters
  R & R Mill Co.
CAPPERS, bottle, (see Bottle cappers)
CAPPUCCINO, (see Coffee makers, cappucino)
CARBOY/bottle rinsers
  Presque Isle Wine Cellars
CARBOYS, wine
  Presque Isle Wine Cellars
CARVING boards
  Butcher Block & More
  Hoffritz
  Horchow Mail Order, Inc.
  Lewis & Conger
  Rosenthal Studio-Haus
  Weston Bowl Mill
CASSEROLES
  E. DeHillerin
  Horchow Mail Order, Inc.
  Lekvar by the Barrel
CASSEROLES, aluminum
  Fashionable
CASSEROLES, cast iron
  Portland Stove Foundry Co.
CASSEROLES, ceramic
  Bennington Potters, Inc.
  Forrest Jones, Inc.
  Lewis & Conger
CASSEROLES, copper
  Bazaar de la Cuisine
  E. DeHillerin
  Greek Island Ltd.
  Lekvar by the Barrel
  Paprikas Weiss Importer
CASSEROLES, electric
  Cornwall Corporation
CASSEROLES, enamel
  Rosenthal Studio-Haus
CASSEROLES, stainless steel
  Finland Design, Inc.
CAULDRONS
  Lekvar by the Barrel
CHAFING dishes
  Bazaar de la Cuisine
CHEESE boards
  Hoffritz
  Holland Handicrafts
  The Left Hand
  Weston Bowl Mill
  Wisconsin Cheese Makers Guild
CHEESE forms
  Holland Handicrafts
CHEESE graters, (see Grinders, cheese)
CHEESE-making kits
  Lewis & Conger
  Maid of Scandinavia Company
CHEESE slicers, (see Slicers, cheese)
CHERRY pitters, (see Pitters, cherry)
CHESTNUT roasters, (see Roasters, chestnut)
CHOCOLATE molds, (see Molds, chocolate)
CHOPPERS, vegetable, (see Vegetable choppers)
CHURNS, electric
  Homestead Industries
  R & R Mill Co.
CIDER presses, (see Presses, cider)
CLAM knives, (see Knives, clam and oyster)
CLAM/oyster openers
  Cross Imports, Inc.
  Hoffritz
  Lewis & Conger
CLAM steamers
  Cross Imports, Inc.
  Lekvar by the Barrel
  Saltwater Farm
CLEAVERS
  Bazaar de la Cuisine
  Cathay Hardware Corp.
  Cross Omports, Inc.
  E. DeHillerin
  Hoffritz
  Horchow Mail Order, Inc.
  Lekvar by the Barrel

Weston Bowl Mill
CODDLERS, (see Egg coddlers)
COFFEE grinders, (see Grinders, coffee)
COFFEE makers
   Bazaar de la Cuisine
   Braun North America
   Chemex Corp.
   Cornwall Corporation
   Cross Imports, Inc.
   Empire Coffee and Tea Company
   Horchow Mail Order, Inc.
   Lekvar by the Barrel
   Lewis & Conger
   Peter Niles Outdoorsman and International Shopper
   Northwestern Coffee Mills
   Paprikas Weiss Importer
   Rosenthal Studio-Haus
   The Smilie Company
   Wisconsin Cheese Makers Guild
COFFEEMAKERS, cappucino
   Lewis & Conger
COFFEEMAKERS, espresso
   Bazzar de la Cuisine
   Cross Imports, Inc.
   Empire Coffee and Tea Company
   Hoffritz
   Horchow Mail Order, Inc.
   Manganaro's Food, Inc.
   Northwestern Coffee Mills
   Paprikas Weiss Importer
COFFEEMAKERS, turkish
   Bazaar de la Cuisine
   Cross Imports, Inc.
   Empire Coffee and Tea Company
   Greek Island Ltd.
   Lekvar by the Barrel
   Northwestern Coffee Mills
   Paprikas Weiss Importer
COFFEE roasters
   Lekvar by the Barrel
COLANDERS
   Bazaar de la Cuisine
   The Blue Owl
   Cross Imports, Inc.
   E. DeHillerin
   Lewis & Conger
   Lillian Vernon Corp.
   Maid of Scandinavia Company
   Miles Kimball
   Paprikas Weiss Importer
COLANDERS, copper
   Bazaar de la Cuisine
   Horchow Mail Order, Inc.
   Lekvar by the Barrel
COOKIE boards
   Holland Handicrafts
COOKIE irons
   Maid of Scandinavia Company
COOKIE molds, (see Molds, cookie)
COOKIE/noodle makers
   Lekvar by the Barrel
   Maid of Scandinavia Company
COOKIE presses, (see Presses, cookie)
COOKIE sheets
   Cake Decorators
   Cross Imports, Inc.
   Maid of Scandinavia Company
   Pfeil & Holing, Inc.
   Wilton Enterprises, Inc.
CORERS, apple, (see Apple corers)
CORK extracters
   Presque Isle Wine Cellars
   Semplex of U.S.A.
CORKING machines
   Winecraft
CORKS
   Cross Imports, Inc.
   Miles Kimball
   Sunset House
CORKS/crowns/caps, wine
   Lekvar by the Barrel
   Presque Isle Wine Cellars
   Semplex of U.S.A.
   Winecraft
CORKSCREWS
   The Aristera Organization
   Bazaar de la Cuisine
   Candle Mill Village
   Cross Imports, Inc.
   Forrest Jones, Inc.
   Hoffritz
   The Left Hand
   Lekvar by the Barrel
   Lillian Vernon Corp.
   Manganaro's Food, Inc.
   Paprikas Weiss Importer
   Presque Isle Wine Cellars
   Semplex of U.S.A.
   Weston Bowl Mill
CORKERS, bottle, (see Bottle corkers)
CORN kernal cutters, (see Cutters, corn kernal)
COUSCOUS cookers

Lekvar by the Barrel
Paprikas Weiss Importer
COVERS & lids, frying, see-thru
   Lillian Vernon Corp.
   Miles Kimball
CREAM makers
   Lewis & Congers
CREAM roll tubes, (see Tubes, cream roll)
CREPE suzette pans, (see Pans, crepe suzette)
CROWNS, (see Corks/crowns/caps wine)
CRULLER, french, (see French cruller)
CRUSHER/stemmers
   Presque Isle Wine Cellars
CRUSHERS, fruit
   Presque Isle Wine Cellars
   Semplex of U.S.A.
CUPS, baba rhum
   Cross Imports, Inc.
CUPS, custard
   Sunset House
CUPS, measuring
   Cake Decorators
   The Left Hand
   Lekvar by the Barrel
   Lillian Vernon Corp.
   Maid of Scandinavia Company
   Paprikas Weiss Importer
   The Smilie Company
CUPS, measuring, copper
   Bazaar de la Cuisine
   Lekvar by the Barrel
CUPS, measuring, glass
   Bazaar de la Cuisine
   Paprikas Weiss Importer
CUPS, measuring, stainless steel
   Bazaar de la Cuisine
   Cross Imports, Inc.
   Hoffritz
CUSTARD cups, (see Cups, custard)
CUTTERS, bear claw
   Maid of Scandinavia Company
CUTTERS, biscuit
   Bazaar de la Cuisine
   Cake Decorators
   Lekvar by the Barrel
   Maid of Scandinavia Company
   Paprikas Weiss Importer
CUTTERS, cake
   Cake Decorators
   Cross Imports, Inc.
   Maid of Scandinavia Company
   Pfeil & Holing, Inc.
CUTTERS, candy
   Cake Decorators
CUTTERS, cole slaw
   Cross Imports, Inc.
   Lekvar by the Barrel
   Maid of Scandinavia Company
CUTTERS, cookie
   Bazaar de la Cuisine
   Cake Decorators
   Cross Imports, Inc.
   E. DeHillerin
   Hoffritz
   Lekvar by the Barrel
   Maid of Scandinavia Company
   Paprikas Weiss Importer
   Pfeil & Holing, Inc.
   Wilton Enterprises, Inc.
CUTTERS, corn kernal
   Maid of Scandinavia Company
   Miles Kimball
   R & R Mill Co.
CUTTERS, floral egg
   Bazaar de la Cuisine
CUTTERS, french fry
   Bazaar de la Cuisine
   Cross Imports, Inc.
   E. DeHillerin
CUTTERS, noodle
   Cake Decorators
   Cross Imports, Inc.
   Lekvar by the Barrel
   Maid of Scandinavia Company
   Manganaro's Food, Inc.
   Paprikas Weiss Importer
CUTTERS, noodle, blades
   Maid of Scandinavia Company
CUTTERS, pastry
   Cake Decorators
   Cross Imports, Inc.
   E. DeHillerin
   Paprikas Weiss Importer
CUTTERS, pineapple
   Lekvar by the Barrel
   Maid of Scandinavia Company
CUTTERS, ravioli
   Bazaar de la Cuisine
   Cake Decorators
   Cross Imports, Inc.
   Lekvar by the Barrel
   Manganaro's Food, Inc.
   Paprikas Weiss Importer
CUTTERS, vegetable
   Lekvar by the Barrel
CUTTERS, tart
   Cake Decorators

Maid of Scandinavia Company
CUTTING boards
  Bazaar de la Cuisine
  Butcher Block & More
  Cross Imports, Inc.
  Fashionable
  Forrest Jones, Inc.
  Hoffritz
  Horchow Mail Order, Inc.
  Lekvar by the Barrel
  Lewis & Conger
  Lillian Vernon Corp.
  Maid of Scandinavia Company
  Miles Kimball
  Rosenthal Studio-Haus
  Sunset House
  Weston Bowl Mill
  Wisconsin Cheese Makers Guild
DECORATING sets, (see Cake decorating sets)
DEEP friers, (see Friers, deep)
DISHES, lasagne, (see Lasagne dishes)
DISHES, soufle, (see Soufle dishes)
DISTILLERS, water, (see Water distillers)
DIVIDERS, cake, (see Cake dividers)
DIVIDERS, dough, (see Dough dividers)
DOCKER rollers, (see Rollers, docker)
DONUT makers
  Cake Decorators
  R & R Mill Co.
  Sunset House
DOUBLE boilers, (see Pans, double boilers)
DOUGH dividers, expansion
  Pfeil & Holing, Inc.
DOUGH kneaders
  Bazaar de la Cuisine
  Cross Imports, Inc.
  Homestead Industries
  Lekvar by the Barrel
  Lewis & Conger
  Magic Mill
  Maid of Scandinavia Company
  Paprikas Weiss Importer
  R & R Mill Co.
  Retsel Inc.
DOUGH scrapers
  Bazaar de la Cuisine
DOUGH thermometers, (see thermometers, dough)

DRIPPING jars
  Lekvar by the Barrel
  Lillian Vernon Corp.
DUCK presses, (see Presses, duck)
DUTCH ovens
  E. DeHillerin
DUTCH ovens, cast iron
  Cross Imports, Inc.
  Lodge Manufacturing Co.
  Paprikas Weiss Importer
  Portland Stove Foundry Co.
  R & R Mill Co.
  The Smilie Company
DUTCH ovens, cast iron, enamelled
  Cross Imports, Inc.
DUTCH ovens, stainless steel
  General Nutrition Corp.
  Homestead Industries
DUTCH ovens, teflon
  Bazaar de la Cuisine
EBELSKIVER pans, (see Pans, ebelskiver)
EBULLIOMETERS
  Presque Isle Wine Cellars
ECLAIR pans, (see Pans, eclair)
EGG coddlers
  Bazaar de la Cuisine
  Hoffritz
  Horchow Mail Order, Inc.
  Lillian Vernon Corp.
EGG cookers
  Sunset House
  Wisconsin Cheese Makers Guild
EGG cutters, (see Cutters, egg)
EGG poachers
  Bazaar de la Cuisine
  The Blue Owl
  Cross Imports, Inc.
  Hoffritz
  Horchow Mail Order, Inc.
  Maid of Scandinavia Company
  Miles Kimball
  Paprikas Weiss Importer
  Sunset House
EGG scissors
  Lewsi & Conger
EGG separators
  Bazaar de la Cuisine
  Hoffritz
  Paprikas Weiss Importer
ESPRESSO, (see Coffeemakers, espresso)
EXTRACTERS, cork, (see Cork extracters)

FERMENTATION containers, plastic
   Semplex of U.S.A.
FERMENTATION locks
   Lekvar by the Barrel
   Presque Isle Wine Cellars
   Semplex of U.S.A.
   Winecraft
FILTERS, water, (see Water filters)
FILTERS, wine, (see Wine filters)
FIREPLACE grates
   Radiant Grate, Inc.
FIREPLACE grills, (see Grills, fireplace)
FIREPLACE ovens
   Radiant Grate, Inc.
FIREPLACE rotisseries
   Radiant Grate, Inc.
FIREPLACE stoves
   Radiant Grate, Inc.
FISH pans, (see Pans, fish)
FISH scalers
   Bazaar de la Cuisine
FLAN rings
   Bazaar de la Cuisine
   Cross Imports, Inc.
   E. DeHillerin
   Lekvar by the Barrel
   Maid of Scandinavia Company
   Paprikas Weiss Importer
FONDANT paddles
   Cake Decorators
FONDUE forks, (see Forks, fondue)
FONDUE pans, (see Pans, fondue)
FORKS, fondue
   Cross Imports, Inc.
   Hoffritz
   Lekvar by the Barrel
FORKS, meat, (giant)
   Bazaar de la Cuisine
   Cross Imports, Inc.
   Lillian Vernon Corp.
   Maid of Scandinavia Company
   Miles Kimball
   Rosenthal Studio-Haus
   Sunset House
FORKS, salad serving
   Horchow Mail Order, Inc.
   Rosenthal Studio-Haus
   Weston Bowl Mill
FORKS, snail
   Cross Imports, Inc.
   Hoffritz
   Horchow Mail Order, Inc.

   Manganaro's Food, Inc.
FORMS, (see Cheese forms)
FRENCH cruller bag sets
   Cake Decorators
   Lekvar by the Barrel
FRENCH fry cutters, (see Cutters, french fry)
FRIERS, deep fat, electric
   Cornwall Corporation
   Paprikas Weiss Importer
FRIERS, deep fat, top of stove
   Cross Imports, Inc.
FRUIT crushers, (see Crushers, fruit)
FRUIT grinders, (see Grinders, fruit or cider presses/fruit grinders)
FRUIT presses, (see Presses, fruit)
FRUIT strainers, (see Strainers, fruit)
FUNNELS
   Bazaar de la Cuisine
   Cake Decorators
   E. DeHillerin
   Lillian Vernon Corp.
   Maid of Scandinavia Company
   Presque Isle Wine Cellars
   Semplex of U.S.A.
   Wilton Enterprises, Inc.
FUNNELS, sausage
   Manganaro's Food, Inc.
GARLIC presses, (see Presses, garlic)
GAUFRETTE irons, (see Irons, gaufrette)
GELATINE molds, (see Molds, gelatine)
GORO irons, (see Irons, goro)
GRAIN mills, (see Grinders, grain)
GRATERS/ slicers
   The Aristera Organization
GRATERS, (see Grinders)
GRIDDLES, aluminum
   Cross Imports, Inc.
   The Smilie Company
GRIDDLES, cast iron
   Cross Imports, Inc.
   Lodge Manufacturing Co.
   R & R Mill Co.
   The Smilie Company
GRIDDLES, electric
   Maid of Scandinavia Company
GRIDDLES, soapstone
   Vermont Soapstone Co., Inc.

GRIDDLES, top of stove
  E. DeHillerin
  Maid of Scandinavia Company
  Paprikas Weiss Importer
  Sunset House
GRILLS, electric
  Paprikas Weiss Importer
GRILLS, fireplace
  Portland Stove Foundry Co.
  Radiant Grate, Inc.
  The Smilie Company
GRILLS, fish
  Hoffritz
GRILLS, top of stove
  Lewis & Conger
  Sunset House
GRINDER/blender combos
  Bissinger's
  Braun North America
  Retsel, Inc.
GRINDER/press combos
  Natural Technology Design
GRINDERS. baby food
  Bowland-Jacobs Manufacturing Co.
  Retsel, Inc.
  Walnut Acres
GRINDERS, cheese
  Bazaar de la Cuisine
  Candle Mill Willage
  Cross Imports, Inc.
  Lekvar by the Barrel
  Lewis & Conger
  Maid of Scandinavia Company
  Manganaro's Food, Inc.
  Miles Kimball
  Paprikas Weiss Importer
  R & R Mill Co.
  Walnut Acres
GRINDERS, chocolate
  Maid of Scandinavia Company
GRINDERS, coffee, electric
  Bazaar de la Cuisine
  Braun North America
  Empire Coffee and Tea Company
  Northwestern Coffee Mills
GRINDERS, coffee, manual
  Candle Mill Village
  Cross Imports, Inc.
  Empire Coffee and Tea Company
  Lekvar by the Barrel
  Maid of Scandinavia Company
  Manganaro's Food, Inc.
  Northwestern Coffee Mills

  Paprikas Weiss Importer
  R & R Mill Co.
GRINDERS, electric
  Bissingers
  Cross Imports, Inc.
  R & R Mill Co.
  Retsel, Inc.
GRINDERS, fruit
  Cross Imports, Inc.
GRINDERS, grain
  General Nutrition Corp.
  Homestead Industries
  R & R Mill Co.
  Walnut Acres
GRINDERS, grain, stone
  Homestead Industries
  Lee Engineering Co.
  Magic Mill
  Meadows Mill Company
  R & R Mill Co.
  Retsel, Inc.
GRINDERS, meat, electric
  Homestead Industries
  Lekvar by the Barrel
  R & R Mill Co.
GRINDERS, meat, manual
  Bazaar de la Cuisine
  Cross Imports, Inc.
  Lekvar by the Barrel
  Paprikas Weiss Importer
GRINDERS, nut
  Lekvar by the Barrel
  Maid of Scandinavia Company
GRINDERS, nutmeg
  Cross Imports, Inc.
  Hoffritz
GRINDERS, rotary
  Candle Mill Village
  Cross Imports, Inc.
  R & R Mill Co.
GRINDERS, salt & pepper
  Bazaar de la Cuisine
  Cross Imports, Inc.
  E. DeHillerin
  Empire Coffee and Tea Company
  Hoffritz
  Horchow Mail Order, Inc.
  Lekvar by the Barrel
  Lewis & Conger
  Lillian Vernon Corp.
  Maid of Scandinavia Company
  Manganaro's Food, Inc.
  Paprikas Weiss Importer
  Rosenthal Studio-Haus
  Weston Bowl Mill

    Wisconsin Cheese Makers Guild
GRINDERS, sausage
    Cross Imports, Inc.
GRINDERS, spice
    Bazaar de la Cuisine
    Lekvar by the Barrel
    Paprikas Weiss Importer
GRINDERS, universal
    Cross Imports, Inc.
    E. DeHillerin
    Lewis & Conger
    R & R Mill Co.
HAMBURGER presses, (see Presses, hamburger)
HAMMERS, steak, (see Steak hammers)
HEARTH reflectors
    Radiant Grate, Inc.
HEAT pads, (see Kitchen heat pads)
HEATERS, immersion, (see Immersion heaters)
HIBACHIS-cast iron
    Lewis & Conger
    Lodge Manufacturing Co.
HOT dog cookers
    Wisconsin Cheese Makers Guild
HYDROMETER jars
    Presque Isle Wine Cellars
HYDROMETERS
    Presque Isle Wine Cellars
    Semplex of U.S.A.
    Winecraft
ICE cream freezers, electric
    Cornwall Corporation
    Homestead Industries
    Maid of Scandinavia Company
    Paprikas Weiss Importer
    White Mountain Freezer, Inc.
ICE cream freezers, manual
    Homestead Industries
    Lillian Vernon Corp.
    R & R Mill Co.
    Sunset House
    White Mountain Freezer, Inc.
ICE cream freezers, refrigerator
    Lewis & Conger
ICE cream molds, (see Molds, ice cream)
ICE cream scoops, (see Scoops, ice cream)
ICE tongs, (see Tongs, ice)
ICING syringes
    Cake Decorators
    Lekvar by the Barrel
    Maid of Scandinavia Company
    Pfeil & Holing, Inc.

IMMERSION heaters
    Lewis & Conger
    Sunset House
INFUSERS, tea, (see Tea infusers)
IRONS, gaufrette
    Cake Decorators
IRONS, goro
    Cake Decorators
IRONS, kromkake
    Cake Decorators
    Cross Imports, Inc.
IRONS, ostia
    Cake Decorators
IRONS, pizzelle
    Cake Decorators
    Cross Imports, Inc.
    Manganaro's Food, Inc.
IRONS, timbale
    Cake Decorators
    Cross Imports, Inc.
    Lekvar by the Barrel
    Maid of Scandinavia Company
    Sunset House
JAGGERS, pie, (see Pie jaggers)
JAR openers, (see also Canning jar lifters)
    Cross Imports, Inc.
    Lewis and Conger
    Miles Kimball
JUICERS
    Bazaar de la Cusine
    Braun North America
    Cross Imports, Inc.
    E. DeHillerin
    General Nutrition Corp.
    Hoffritz
    Homestead Industries
    Juice Master Manufacturing Company
    Lekvar by the Barrel
    Lewis & Conger
    Miles Kimball
    Paprikas Weiss Importer
    R & R Mill Co.
    Sunset House
JUICERS, steam
    A.V. Food Co.
KETTLES, water, (see Water kettles)
KITCHEN heat pads
    Daisyfresh Yogurt Company
KNEADERS, dough, (see Dough kneaders)
KNIFE/fork combos
    Hoffritz
    The Left Hand

KNIFE sharpeners
   Bazaar de la Cuisine
   Hoffritz
   Maid of Scandinavia Company
   Weston Bowl Mill
KNIFE sharpeners, butcher's steel
   Cross Imports, Inc.
   Hoffritz
   Liberty Organization
   Weston Bowl Mill
KNIVES, bread
   The Aristera Organization
   Bazaar de la Cuisine
   Cross Imports, Inc.
   Hoffritz
KNIVES, cake
   Hoffritz
   The Left Hand
   Maid of Scandinavia Company
   Wilton Enterprises, Inc.
KNIVES, carbon steel
   Bazaar de la Cuisine
   Cross Imports, Inc.
   E. DeHillerin
   Hoffritz
   Lekvar by the Barrel
   Liberty Organization
   Paprikas Weiss Importer
   Weston Bowl Mill
KNIVES, clam & oyster
   Bazaar de la Cuisine
   Cross Imports, Inc.
   Hoffritz
   Paprikas Weiss Importer
KNIVES, rustproof steel
   Liberty Organization
KNIVES, stainless steel
   Bazaar de la Cuisine
   Forrest Jones, Inc.
   Hoffritz
   Horchow Mail Order, Inc.
   The Left Hand
   Lewis & Conger
   Pfeil & Holing, Inc.
   Rosenthal Studio-Haus
KNIVES, vanadium steel
   Sunset House
KRIMP cut sealers
   Bazaar de la Cuisine
   Lekvar by the Barrel
   Maid of Scandinavia Company
   Paprikas Weiss Importer
LADLES
   The Aristera Organization
   Bazaar de la Cuisine
   Cathay Hardware Corp.
   Cross Imports, Inc.
   The Left Hand
   Lekvar by the Barrel
   Maid of Scandinavia Company
   Rosenthal Studio-Haus
   The Smilie Company
   Weston Bowl Mill
LARDING needles
   Bazaar de la Cuisine
   Cross Imports, Inc.
   Lekvar by the Barrel
   Paprikas Weiss Importer
LASAGNE dishes
   Bennington Potters, Inc.
   Lewis & Conger
LEMON wedge squeezers
   Bazaar de la Cuisine
   Maid of Scandinavia Company
   Paprikas Weiss Importer
LIDS, (see Covers)
LIDS, sprouter, (see Sprouter lids)
LIFTERS, (see also Poultry lifters)
   The Smilie Company
LIFTERS, steel
   The Smilie Company
MASHERS, potato, (see Potato mashers)
MEASURING cups, (see Cups, measuring)
MEASURING spoons, (see Spoons, measuring)
MEAT ball presses, (see Presses, meat ball)
MEAT forks, (see Forks, meat)
MEAT grinders, (see Grinders, meat)
MEAT saws
   Cross Imports, Inc.
   E. DeHillerin
   Retsel, Inc.
MEAT slicers, (see Slicers, meat)
MEAT thermometers, (see Thermometers, meat)
MESS kits
   The Smilie Company
MILLS, (see Grinders)
MINCERS
   Bazaar de la Cuisine
   Hoffritz
   Lekvar by the Barrel
   Lewis & Conger
   Maid of Scandinavia Company
   Paprikas Weiss Importer
MIXERS, electric

Magic Mill
Retsel, Inc.
MIXING bowls, (see Bowls, mixing)
MIXING spoons, (see Spoons, mixing)
MOLDS, aluminum
  Paprikas Weiss Importer
MOLDS, butter
  Bazaar de la Cuisine
  Holland Handicrafts
  Lekvar by the Barrel
  Paprikas Weiss Importer
  Weston Bowl Mill
MOLDS, cake
  Bazaar de la Cuisine
  Cake Decorators
  Cross Imports, Inc.
  E. DeHillerin
  Lekvar by the Barrel
  Maid of Scandinavia Company
  Paprikas Weiss Importer
  Pfeil & Holing, Inc.
  Wilton Enterprises, Inc.
MOLDS, candy
  Cake Decorators
  Lekvar by the Barrel
  Maid of Scandinavia Company
  Wilton Enterprises, Inc.
MOLDS, chocolate
  Cake Decorators
  E. DeHillerin
  Holland Handicrafts
  Lekvar by the Barrel
  Pfeil & Holing, Inc.
  Wilton Enterprises, Inc.
MOLDS, cookie
  Cross Imports, Inc.
  Holland Handicrafts
  Maid of Scandinavia Company
MOLDS, copper
  Bazaar de la Cuisine
  Lekvar by the Barrel
MOLDS, gelatine
  Bazaar de la Cuisine
  Cake Decorators
  Cross Imports, Inc.
  E. DeHillerin
  Lekvar by the Barrel
  Maid of Scandinavia Company
  Pfeil & Holing, Inc.
  Wilton Enterprises, Inc.
MOLDS, ice cream
  Cake Decorators
  Cross Imports, Inc.
  Lekvar by the Barrel
  Maid of Scandinavia Company
  Pfeil & Holing, Inc.
  Wilton Enterprises, Inc.
MOLDS, pate
  Bazaar de la Cuisine
  Cross Imports, Inc.
  E. DeHillerin
  Paprikas Weiss Importer
MOLDS, sugar
  Cake Decorators
  Wilton Enterprises, Inc.
MOLDS, tart
  Cake Decorators
  Lekvar by the Barrel
  Maid of Scandinavia Company
  Pfeil & Holing, Inc.
MORTARS & pestles, brass
  Hoffritz
  Lekvar by the Barrel
MORTARS & pestles, ceramic
  Lillian Vernon Corp.
MORTARS & pestles, wood
  Bazaar de la Cuisine
  Cake Decorators
  Cross Imports, Inc.
  Lekvar by the Barrel
  Lillian Vernon Corp.
  Maid of Scandinavia Company
  Weston Bowl Mill
MUFFIN pans, (see Pans, muffin)
MUSTACHE spoons, (see Spoons, mustache)
NEEDLES, (see Lading needles)
NESTING pans, (see Pans, nesting)
NOODLE boards
  Lekvar by the Barrel
  Paprikas Weiss Importer
NOODLE cutters, (see Cutters, noodle)
NOODLE making machines (see also cookie/noodle makers and pasta machines)
  Cake Decorators
  Cross Imports, Inc.
  Horchow Mail Order, Inc.
  Maid of Scandinavia Company
  Manganaro's Food, Inc.
NUT grinders, (see Grinders, nut)
NUTCRACKERS
  Hoffritz
  Weston Bowl Mill
NUTMEG grinders, (see Grinders, nutmeg)
OMELET pans, (see Pans, omelet)

OVEN/broilers
　Cornwall Corporation
ONION presses, (see Presses, onion)
ORNAMENTS, (see Cake Ornaments)
OSTIA irons, (see Irons, ostia)
OVEN forks, (see Forks, oven)
OVENS, fireplace, (see Fireplace ovens)
OVEN spades
　Lillian Vernon Corp.
　Maid of Scandinavia Company
　Pfeil & Holing, Inc.
OVEN thermometers, (see Thermometers, oven)
OYSTER knives, (see Knives, clam and oyster)
OYSTER openers, (see Clam/oyster openers)
PAN strainers, (see Strainers, pan)
PANS, asparagus boiler
　Bazaar de la Cuisine
　Cross Imports, Inc.
　Horc ow Mail Order, Inc.
　Lekvar by the Barrel
　Lewis & Conger
PANS, au gratin
　Lekvar by the Barrel
PANS, au gratin, enamel
　Lekvar by t e Barrel
PANS, baking, ceramic
　Bazaar de la Cuisine
PANS, baking, enamel
　Lekvar by t e Barrel
PANS, baking, stainless steel
　Cross Imports, Inc.
　Maid of Scandinavia Company
PANS, blancher-canning
　Miles Kimball
PANS, bread
　Bazaar de la Cuisine
　Cross Imports, Inc.
　Lekvar by the Barrel
　Maid of Scandinavia Company
　Pfeil & Holing, Inc.
　Walnut Acres
PANS, bread, cast iron
　Lodge Manufacturing Co.
PANS, bread, ceramic
　Bennington Potters, Inc.
PANS, broiler
　Cross Imports, Inc.
　Fashionable
　Lillian Vernon Corp.
　Maid of Scandinavia Company
　Miles Kimball
　Sunset House
　Walnut Acres
　Wisconsin Cheese Makers Guild
PANS, cake
　Bazaar de la Cuisine
　Cake Decorators
　Cross Imports, Inc.
　Maid of Scandinavia Company
　Miles Kimball
　Paprikas Weiss Importer
　Pfeil & Holing, Inc.
　Sunset House
　Wilton Enterprises, Inc.
PANS, cake, springform
　Bazaar de la Cuisine
　Cake Decorators
　Cross Imports, Inc.
　Lekvar by the Barrel
　Maid of Scandinavia Company
　Pfeil & Holing, Inc.
PANS, crepe suzette
　Bazaar de la Cuisine
　Cross Imports, Inc.
　Horchow Mail Order, Inc.
　Paprikas Weiss Importer
PANS, crepe suzette, copper
　Bazaar de la Cuisine
PANS, crepe suzette, enamel
　Lekvar by the Barrel
PANS, double boilers
　Cross Imports, Inc.
　Lekvar by the Barrel
　Maid of Scandinavia Company
　Paprikas Weiss Importer
PANS, double boiler, copper
　Horchow Mail Order, Inc.
　Lekvar by the Barrel
PANS, ebleskiver
　Cake Decorators
　Cross Imports, Inc.
　Paprikas Weiss Importer
PANS, eclair
　Cake Decorators
　Lekvar by the Barrel
　Maid of Scandinavia Company
　Paprikas Weiss Importer
PANS, enamelled cast iron
　Cross Imports, Inc.
　Forrest Jones, Inc.
　Lekvar by the Barrel
PANS, fish boiler
　Bazaar de la Cuisine
　Cross Imports, Inc.
　E. DeHillerin
　Horchow Mail Order, Inc.

Lekvar by the Barrel
Paprikas Weiss Importer
PANS, fondue
  The Blue Owl
  Cross Imports, Inc.
  E. DeHillerin
  Finland Design, Inc.
  Maid of Scandinavia Company
PANS, fondue, cast iron
  Rosenthal Studio-Haus
PANS, fondue, copper
  Lekvar by the Barrel
  Paprikas Weiss Importer
PANS, fondue, electric
  Cornwall Corporation
  Wisconsin Cheese Makers Guild
PANS, fry
  Cross Imports, Inc.
PANS, fry, aluminum
  Cross Imports, Inc.
  Paprikas Weiss Importer
  The Smilie Company
PANS, fry, cast iron
  Cross Imports, Inc.
  Lodge Manufacturing Co.
  Paprikas Weiss Importer
  Portland Stove Foundry Co.
PANS, fry, copper
  Bazaar de la Cuisine
  E. DeHillerin
  Lekvar by the Barrel
  Paprikas Weiss Importer
PANS, fry, enamel
  Rosenthal Studio-Haus
PANS, fry, stainless steel
  Homestead Industries
PANS, fry, steel
  Lekvar by the Barrel
  The Smilie Company
PANS, fry, teflon
  Bazaar de la Cuisine
  Cross Imports, Inc.
  The Smilie Company
PANS, lasagne
  Horchow Mail Order, Inc.
PANS, muffin
  Bazaar de la Cuisine
  Cake Decorators
  Cross Imports, Inc.
  Maid of Scandinavia Company
  Pfeil & Holing, Inc.
  Wilton Enterprises, Inc.
PANS, muffin, cast iron
  Lodge Manufacturing Co.
  Paprikas Weiss Importer
  Portland Stove Foundry Co.

PANS, nesting
  The Smilie Company
PANS, omelet
  Bazaar de la Cuisine
  Cross Imports, Inc.
  E. DeHillerin
  Horchow Mail Order, Inc.
  Lekvar by the Barrel
  Lewis & Conger
  Lillian Vernon Corp.
  Maid of Scandinavia Company
  Paprikas Weiss Importer
  Wisconsin Cheese Makers Guild
PANS, omelet, cast iron
  Cross Imports, Inc.
PANS, pie
  Cake Decorators
  Cross Imports, Inc.
  Maid of Scandinavia Company
  Pfeil & Holing, Inc.
PANS, pie, ceramic
  Bennington Potters, Inc.
PANS, pizza
  Cross Imports, Inc.
  Maid of Scandinavia Company
PANS, roasting
  Cross Imports, Inc.
  Miles Kimball
PANS, roasting, stainless steel
  Bazaar de la Cuisine
PANS, sauce
  Cross Imports, Inc.
  E. DeHillerin
  Lewis & Conger
  Miles Kimball
PANS, sauce, aluminum
  Paprikas Weiss Importer
PANS, sauce, cast iron
  Lodge Manufacturing Co.
  Paprikas Weiss Importer
  Portland Stove Foundry Co.
PANS, sauce, copper
  Bazaar de la Cuisine
  E. DeHillerin
  Horchow Mail Order, Inc.
  Lekvar by the Barrel
  Paprikas Weiss Importer
PANS, sauce, enamel
  Rosenthal Studio-Haus
PANS, sauce, glass
  Horchow Mail Order, Inc.
PANS, sauce, stainless steel
  Finland Design, Inc.
  General Nutrition Corp.
  Homestead Industries

PANS, sauce, teflon
   Bazaar de la Cuisine
PANS, strudel
   Lekvar by the Barrel
PANS, tart
   Cross Imports, Inc.
PASTA machines, (see also Noodle making machines)
   Bazaar de la Cuisine
PASTRY brushes
   Bazaar de la Cuisine
   Cross Imports, Inc.
   E. DeHillerin
   Paprikas Weiss Importer
PASTRY cutters, (see Cutters, pastry)
PASTRY rollers, (see Rollers, pastry)
PASTRY tubes, (see Tubes, pastry)
PATE molds, (see Molds, pate)
PEELERS
   The Aristera Organization
   Bazaar de la Cuisine
   Cross Imports, Inc.
   Fashionable
   Hoffritz
   The Left Hand
   Maid of Scandinavia Company
   Miles Kimball
PEELERS, apple (see also Apple corers)
   Cake Decorators
PESTLES, (see Mortars and pestles)
PICKLING kits
   Bazaar de la Cuisine
PIE birds
   Candle Mill Village
   Hoffritz
   Horchow Mail Order, Inc.
PIE jaggers
   Cake Decorators
   Maid of Scandinavia Company
   Pfeil & Holing, Inc.
PIE pans, (see Pans, pie)
PINCHCOCKS
   Presque Isle Wine Cellars
PINEAPPLE cutters, (see Cutters, pineapple)
PINS, roasting, (see Roasting pins)
PITTERS, cherry
   Bazaar de la Cuisine
   Cake Decorators
   Hoffritz
   Lekvar by the Barrel
   Paprikas Weiss Importer
   R & R Mill Co.
PITTERS, plum
   Pfeil & Holing, Inc.
PIZZA pans, (see Pans, pizza)
PIZZELLE irons, (see Irons, pizzelle)
POACHERS, (see Egg poachers)
POPCORN poppers
   Cornwall Corporation
   Cross Imports, Inc.
   Lekvar by the Barrel
   Wisconsin Cheese Makers Guild
POP-UP toasters, (see Toasters, pop-up)
POTATO cutters, (see Cutters, french fries)
POTATO mashers
   Lekvar by the Barrel
   Weston Bowl Mill
POTS, (see also Pans or specific type of pot, i.e. Bean pots)
POULTRY lifters
   Cross Imports, Inc.
POULTRY shears, (see Shears, poultry)
PRESSES, (see also Grinder/press combos)
PRESSES, burger
   Cake Decorators
   Cross Imports, Inc.
   Hoffritz
   Maid of Scandinavia Company
PRESSES, butter
   Lekvar by the Barrel
PRESSES, cider, (see Cider presses/fruit grinders)
PRESSES, cookie
   Cake Decorators
   Cross Imports, Inc.
   Lekvar by the Barrel
   Maid of Scandinavia Company
   Wilton Enterprises, Inc.
PRESSES, duck
   Bazaar de la Cuisine
   E. DeHillerin
   Paprikas Weiss Importer
PRESSES, fruit
   Paprikas Weiss Importer
   Presque Isle Wine Cellars
   Semplex of U.S.A.
PRESSES, fruit/vegetable
   R & R Mill Co.
PRESSES, garlic
   Bazaar de la Cuisine
   The Blue Owl

Cross Imports, Inc.
Lekvar by the Barrel
Maid of Scandinavia Company
Manganaro's Food, Inc.
Miles Kimball
Paprikas Weiss Importer
PRESSES, meat ball
　The Blue Owl
PRESSES, onion
　Paprikas Weiss Importer
PRESSURE cookers
　R & R Mill Co.
　Retsel, Inc.
PUDDING forms, (see Steam pudding forms)
PURIFIERS, water, (see Water purifiers)
RACKS, roasting, (see Roasting racks or steam racks)
RACKS, broiler, (see Broiler racks)
RAVIOLI cutters, (see Cutters, ravioli)
RAVIOLI rollers, (see Rollers, ravioli)
REFLECTORS, hearth, (see Hearth reflectors)
RICE balls
　Horchow Mail Order, Inc.
RICE steamers
　Cross Imports, Inc.
RICERS
　Bazaar de la Cuisine
　Cross Imports, Inc.
　Lekvar by the Barrel
　Paprikas Weiss Importer
　R & R Mill Co.
ROAST holders
　Lillian Vernon Corp.
ROASTERS, chestnut
　Bazaar de la Cuisine
ROASTING pans, (see Pans, roasting)
ROASTING pins
　Lewis & Conger
ROASTING racks
　Cross Imports, Inc.
　Lewis & Conger
　Maid of Scandinavia Company
ROLLERS, docker
　E. DeHillerin
　Maid of Scandinavia Company
　Pfeil & Holing, Inc.
ROLLERS, pastry
　Cross Imports, Inc.
　Maid of Scandinavia Company

Pfeil & Holing, Inc.
ROLLERS, ravioli
　Cross Imports, Inc.
　Manganaro's Food, Inc.
ROLLERS, springerle cookie
　The Blue Owl
　Cake Decorators
　Lekvar by the Barrel
　Paprikas Weiss Importer
　Pfeil & Holing, Inc.
　Weston Bowl Mill
ROLLING pins
　Bazaar de la Cuisine
　Cross Imports, Inc.
　Lekvar by the Barrel
　Paprikas Weiss Importer
　Pfeil & Holing, Inc.
　Weston Bowl Mill
ROTISSERIES, (see Broilers, rotisseries)
ROTISSERIES, fireplace, (see Fireplace rotisseries)
ROTISSERIE thermometers, (see Thermometers, rotisserie)
RUBBER stoppers, (see Stoppers, rubber)
SALAD baskets
　Bazaar de la Cuisine
　Cross Imports, Inc.
　E. DeHillerin
　Lekvar by the Barrel
　Sunset House
SALAD forks, (see Forks, salad)
SALAD tongs, (see Tongs, salad)
SALT and pepper grinders, (see Grinders, salt and pepper)
SAUCE pans, (see Pans, sauce)
SAUSAGE funnels, (see Funnels, sausage)
SAUSAGE grinders, (see Grinders, sausage)
SAUSAGE making kits
　Maid of Scandinavia Company
SAUSAGE stuffers
　Cross Imports, Inc.
　Homestead Industries
　Lekvar by the Barrel
　Maid of Scandinavia Company
　Paprikas Weiss Importer
　R & R Mill Co.
SAWS, meat, (see Meat saws)
SCALERS, (see Fish scalers)
SCALES
　Cake Decorators
　Candle Mill Village
　Cross Imports, Inc.

71

   E. DeHillerin
   Hoffritz
   Horchow Mail Order, Inc.
   Lekvar by the Barrel
   Lewis & Conger
   Maid of Scandinavia Company
   Pfeil & Holing, Inc.
   Presque Isle Wine Cellars
   Walnut Acres
SCOOPS, aluminum
   The Blue Owl
   Maid of Scandinavia Company
   Pfeil & Holing, Inc.
SCOOPS, ice-cream
   The Aristera Organization
   Cross Imports, Inc.
   E. DeHillerin
   Hoffritz
   Horchow Mail Order, Inc.
   The Left Hand
   Maid of Scandinavia Company
   Pfeil & Holing, Inc.
SCOOPS, plastic
   Pfeil & Holing, Inc.
SCOOPS, wooden
   Hoffritz
   Maid of Scandinavia Company
   Weston Bowl Mill
SCRAPERS, dough, (see Dough scrapers)
SEAFOOD shell crackers
   Bazaar de la Cuisine
   Cross Imports, Inc.
   Hoffritz
   Horchow Mail Order, Inc.
SEALERS, (see Can openers)
SEPARATORS, egg (see Egg separators)
SHARPENERS, (see Knife sharpeners)
SHEARS
   Bazaar de la Cuisine
   Hoffritz
   Lewis & Conger
   Saltwater Farm
SHEARS, poultry
   The Blue Owl
   Hoffritz
   Horchow Mail Order, Inc.
   Paprikas Weiss Importer
SHELL crackers, (see Seafood shell crackers)
SHELLERS, shrimp, (see Shrimp shellers)
SHISH kebab sets
   Lillian Vernon Corp.

SHREDDERS, (see Slicers/shredders)
SHRIMP shellers
   Cross Imports, Inc.
   Lekvar by the Barrel
   Paprikas Weiss Importer
SIFTERS
   Cross Imports, Inc.
SIPHONS
   Presque Isle Wine Cellars
SKEWERS
   Bazaar de la Cuisine
   Cake Decorators
   Cross Imports, Inc.
   Hoffritz
   Lekvar by the Barrel
   Maid of Scandinavia Company
SKILLETS
   Cross Imports, Inc.
SKILLETS, cast iron
   Cross Imports, Inc.
   General Nutrition Corp.
   Lodge Manufacturing Co.
   R & R Mill Co.
SKILLETS, partitioned
   Cross Imports, Inc.
   Fashionable
   Lewis & Conger
   Maid of Scandinavia Company
   Miles Kimball
   Sunset House
SKIMMERS
   Cathay Hardware Corp.
   Cross Imports, Inc.
   Paprikas Weiss Importer
SLICERS
   Bazaar de la Cuisine
   Braun North America
   Cross Imports, Inc.
   Lekvar by the Barrel
   Lewis & Conger
   Maid of Scandinavia Company
   Paprikas Weiss Importer
   R & R Mill Co.
   Sunset House
   Weston Bowl Mill
SLICERS, bean
   Bazaar de la Cuisine
   Lekvar by the Barrel
   Lewis & Conger
   Paprikas Weiss Importer
   R & R Mill Co.
SLICERS, cake
   Maid of Scandinavia Company
   Pfeil & Holing, Inc.

SLICERS, cheese
   Cross Imports, Inc.
   Hoffritz
   Horchow Mail Order, Inc.
   Maid of Scandinavia Company
   Walnut Acres
SLICERS, meat
   Lekvar by the Barrel
   Maid of Scandinavia Company
SLICERS, shredders
   Lillian Vernon Corp.
   Miles Kimball
   Paprikas Weiss Importer
   R & R Mill Co.
   Weston Bowl Mill
SMOKERS, electric
   Lewis & Conger
SNAIL dishes
   Bazaar de la Cuisine
   Bennington Potters, Inc.
   Cross Imports, Inc.
   Hoffritz
   Horchow Mail Order, Inc.
   Lekvar by the Barrel
SNAIL dough makers
   Lekvar by the Barrel
SNAIL forks, (see Forks, snail)
SNAIL tongs, (see Tongs, snail)
SOUFFLE dishes
   Bennington Potters, Inc.
   The Blue Owl
   Horchow Mail Order, Inc.
   Lekvar by the Barrel
   Lillian Vernon Corp.
   Maid of Scandinavia Company
   Paprikas Weiss Importer
   Rosenthal Studio-Haus
SPADES, (see Oven spades)
SPAETZLE machines
   Cross Imports, Inc.
   Lekvar by the Barrel
SPATULAS
   Cake Decorators
   Cross Imports, Inc.
   E. DeHillerin
   Maid of Scandinavia Company
   Wilton Enterprises, Inc.
SPATULAS, stainless steel
   Bazaar de la Cuisine
   Cross Imports, Inc.
   Hoffritz
   Lekvar by the Barrel
   Maid of Scandinavia Company
   Miles Kimball
   Paprikas Weiss Importer
   Pfeil & Holing, Inc.

SPATULAS, wood
   Cross Imports, Inc.
   Paprikas Weiss Importer
SPICE racks, wood
   Lillian Vernon Corp.
SPIGOTS, wood
   Lekvar by the Barrel
   Semplex of U.S.A.
SPOONS, long
   The Blue Owl
   Paprikas Weiss Importer
   Semplex of U.S.A.
SPOONS, measuring
   Bazaar de la Cuisine
   Cross Imports, Inc.
   Maid of Scandinavia Company
   Pfeil & Holing, Inc.
SPOONS, mixing
   Bazaar de la Cuisine
   Cross Imports, Inc.
   Forrest Jones, Inc.
   Lekvar by the Barrel
   Lillian Vernon Corp.
   Maid of Scandinavia Company
   Paprikas Weiss Importer
   Pfeil & Holing, Inc.
   Weston Bowl Mill
SPOONS, mustache
   The Left Hand
   Lewis & Conger
SPRINGERLE boards
   Lekvar by the Barrel
   Maid of Scandinavia Company
SPRINGERLE cookie rollers, (see Rollers, springerle cookie)
SPROUTER lids
   Dharma Products
SPROUTERS
   Miles Kimball
   Walnut Acres
SPROUTERS, animal shapes
   Lillian Vernon Corp.
   Sunset House
SPROUTERS, plastic
   Candle Mill Village
   Retsel, Inc.
SQUEEZERS, lemon, (see Lemon squeezers)
STANDS, cake
   Cake Decorators
   Lekvar by the Barrel
   Maid of Scandinavia Company
   Pfeil & Holing, Inc.
   Wilton Enterprises, Inc.
STEAMERS, (see Clam steamers)

STEAK hammers
   Bazaar de la Cuisine
   Cross Imports, Inc.
   Hoffritz
   Lekvar by the Barrel
   Paprikas Weiss Importer
   Weston Bowl Mill
STEAM baskets
   Bazaar de la Cuisine
   Cathay Hardware Corp.
   Cross Imports, Inc.
   Hoffritz
   Horchow Mail Order, Inc.
   Lekvar by the Barrel
   Lewis & Conger
   Paprikas Weiss Importer
   R & R Mill Co.
   Walnut Acres
STEAM baskets, bamboo
   Cathay Hardware Corp.
STEAM pudding forms
   Bazaar de la Cuisine
   Lekvar by the Barrel
   Maid of Scandinavia Company
   Paprikas Weiss Importer
STEAM racks
   Lillian Vernon Corp.
   Sunset House
STEAMERS, rice, (see Rice steamers)
STEMMERS, (see Crusher/stemmer)
STOCK pots
   Cross Imports, Inc.
   E. DeHillerin
   Paprikas Weiss Importer
STOPPERS, plastic
   Semplex of U.S.A.
STOPPERS, rubber
   Presque Isle Wine Cellars
   Semplex of U.S.A.
STOVES, camp
   Retsel, Inc.
   The Smilie Company
STOVES, coal/wood
   Nordic Stove Shoppe-Viking Homestead
   Portland Stove Foundry Co.
   R & R Mill Co.
   Retsel, Inc.
STOVES, fireplace, (see Fireplace stoves)
STRAINERS, extra fine mesh
   Cross Imports, Inc.
STRAINERS, fruits/vegetable
   Bazaar de la Cuisine
   Cross Imports, Inc.
   E. DeHillerin
   Homestead Industries
   Lekvar by the Barrel
   Lewis & Conger
   Maid of Scandinavia Company
   Miles Kimball
   R & R Mill Co.
STRAINERS, pan
   Hoffritz
STRAINERS, tea
   Bazaar de la Cuisine
   Cross Imports, Inc.
   Lekvar by the Barrel
   Paprikas Weiss Importer
STRAINERS, tomato
   Cross Imports, Inc.
   Manganaro's Food, Inc.
   Paprikas Weiss Importer
STRUDEL pans, (see Pans, strudel)
SUGAR molds, (see Molds, sugar)
SUGAR testing kits, wine
   Presque Isle Wine Cellars
SULPHUR locks
   Semplex of U.S.A.
SYRINGES, icing, (see Icing syringes)
TART cutters, (see Cutters, tart)
TART molds, (see Molds, tart)
TART pans, (see Pans, tart)
TEA infusers
   Bazaar de la Cuisine
   Cross Imports, Inc.
   Hoffritz
   Horchow Mail Order, Inc.
   Lillian Vernon Corp.
   Miles Kimball
   Northwestern Coffee Mills
   Paprikas Weiss Importer
TEA strainers, (see Strainers, tea)
TEMPURA cookers, (see Japanese tempura cookers)
THERMOMETER forks
   Maid of Scandinavia Company
THERMOMETER fry baskets
   Bazaar de la Cuisine
THERMOMETERS
   Bazaar de la Cuisine
   Cake Decorators
   Maid of Scandinavia Company
   Presque Isle Wine Cellars
   Semplex of U.S.A
THERMOMETERS, alcohol
   Lekvar by the Barrel
THERMOMETERS, candy
   Bazaar de la Cuisine
   Cake Decorators

Cross Imports, Inc.
Maid of Scandinavia Company
THERMOMETERS, dough
Maid of Scandinavia Company
THERMOMETERS, freezer/refrigerator)
Cross Imports, Inc.
THERMOMETERS, meat
Bazaar de la Cuisine
Cross Imports, Inc.
Maid of Scandinavia Company
THERMOMETERS, oven
Bazaar de la Cuisine
Cake Decorators
Cross Imports, Inc.
TIES, meat, (see Meat ties)
TIMBALE irons, (see Irons, timbale)
TIMERS
Bazaar de la Cuisine
Cake Decorators
Hoffritz
Horchow Mail Order, Inc.
Maid of Scandinavia Company
TOASTER/broilers
Wisconsin Cheese Makers Guild
TOASTERS, pop-up
Braun North America
TOASTERS, sandwich
Cross Imports, Inc.
Paprikas Weiss Importer
TOMATO strainers, (see Strainers tomato)
TONGS
Cross Imports, Inc.
Hoffritz
Horchow Mail Order, Inc.
Lillian Vernon Corp.
Maid of Scandinavia Company
Manganaro's Food, Inc.
Miles Kimball
Pfeil & Holing, Inc.
TONGS, ice
Cross Imports, Inc.
Hoffritz
TONGS, salad
Bazaar de la Cuisine
Cross Imports, Inc.
Hoffritz
Miles Kimball
Weston Bowl Mill
TONGS, snail
Cross Imports, Inc.
Hoffritz
Horchow Mail Order, Inc.
Manganaro's Food, Inc.

TONGS, wooden
Bazaar de la Cuisine
Hoffritz
TUBES, cake decorating
Bazaar de la Cuisine
Cake Decorators
Cross Imports, Inc.
Lekvar by the Barrel
Maid of Scandinavia Company
Pfeil & Holing, Inc.
Wilton Enterprises, Inc.
TUBES, cannoli
Bazaar de la Cuisine
Cake Decorators
Cross Imports, Inc.
Lekvar by the Barrel
Maid of Scandinavia Company
Manganaro's Food, Inc.
Paprikas Weiss Importer
TUBES, cream roll
Cake Decorators
Cross Imports, Inc.
Lekvar by the Barrel
Maid of Scandinavia Company
TUBES, pastry
Cake Decorators
Cross Imports, Inc.
E. DeHillerin
Lekvar by the Barrel
Maid of Scandinavia Company
UTENSIL sets
Bazaar de la Cuisine
Fashionable
Hoffritz
Rosenthal Studio-Haus
UTENSIL sets, copper
Lekvar by the Barrel
UTENSIL sets, melamine
Maid of Scandinavia Company
UTENSIL sets, nylon
Maid of Scandinavia Company
UTENSIL sets, stainless steel
E. DeHillerin
Hoffritz
UTENSIL sets, wood
The Blue Owl
Cross Imports, Inc.
Hoffritz
Lekvar by the Barrel
Lillian Vernon Corp.
Maid of Scandinavia Company
Sunset House
VEGETABLE choppers
Cross Imports, Inc.
VEGETABLE presses, (see Presses, vegetable)

VEGETABLE strainers, (see Strainers, vegetable)
VINOMETERS
   Presque Isle Wine Cellars
   Semplex of U.S.A.
WAFFLE irons, Scandinavian
   Maid of Scandinavia Company
   Paprikas Weiss Importer
WAFFLE irons, top of stove
   Cross Imports, Inc.
   Lekvar by the Barrel
   Maid of Scandinavia Company
WATER distillers
   Clean Water Society
   Cumberland Associates
   R & R Mill Co.
WATER filters
   General Nutrition Corp.
   Lewis & Conger
   Walnut Acres
WATER kettles
   Retsel, Inc.
WATER kettles, brass
   Hoffritz
WATER kettles, copper
   Hoffritz
   Lekvar by the Barrel
   R & R Mill Co.
WATER kettles, enamel
   Cross Imports, Inc.
WATER kettles, glass
   Chemex Corp.
WATER kettles, stainless steel
   Finland Design, Inc.
WATER purifiers
   General Nutrition Corp.
   Lewis & Conger
   Walnut Acres
WHIPS
   Bazaar de la Cuisine
   Cake Decorators
   Cross Imports, Inc.
   E. DeHillerin
   Lekvar by the Barrel
   Maid of Scandinavia Company
   Pfeil & Holing, Inc.
WHISKS
   Cross Imports, Inc.
   Horchow Mail Order, Inc.
   Lekvar by the Barrel
   Lillian Vernon Corp.
   Maid of Scandinavia Company
WHIPPERS, charger
   E. DeHillerin
   Maid of Scandinavia Company
WINE bottles, (see Bottles, wine)

WINE filters
   Presque Isle Wine Cellars
   Semplex of U.S.A.
   Winecraft
WINE-MAKING kits
   Lekvar by the Barrel
   Maid of Scandinavia Company
   Presque Isle Wine Cellars
   Winecraft
WINE thieves
   Presque Isle Wine Cellars
   Semplex of U.S.A.
WOKS
   The Blue Owl
   Cathay Hardware Corp.
   Miles Kimball
WOKS, electric
   Cornwall Corporation
WOKS, stainless steel
   Lillian Vernon Corp.
WOKS, steel
   Bazaar de la Cuisine
   Cross Imports, Inc.
   Horchow Mail Order, Inc.
   Lekvar by the Barrel
   Maid of Scandinavia Company
YOGURT making equipment
   Daisyfresh Yogurt Company
   General Nutrition Corp.
   Lewis & Conger
   Maid of Scandinavia Company
   Walnut Acres
YOGURT making kits
   Semplex of U.S.A.

# OLIVER PRESS

## Presents the Finder's Guide Series

# KITS & PLANS

**FINDER'S GUIDE No. 1**

*Joseph Rosenbloom*

This book offers the do-it-yourselfer a complete directory of companies and equipment available for many diversified projects and plans. This indexed directory solves the problem of finding out "who" makes "what." There is something here for every taste and level of skill.

288 pp
LC 73-92459          $3.95

**Kits and Plans for the Budget Minded**

# CRAFT SUPPLIES SUPERMARKET

### FINDER'S GUIDE No. 2

*Joseph Rosenbloom*

A well illustrated and indexed directory of craft supplies. Thousands of products, including materials, kits, tools, etc., from over 450 companies, are analyzed from their catalogs.

224 pp, ill., August, 1974
LC 74-84298     $3.95

# HOMEGROWN ENERGY

**FINDER'S GUIDE No. 4**

Power for the Home and Homestead

*Gary Wade*

This book offers the do-it-yourselfer a very complete directory to thousands of available products involved in the production of home grown power. Water wheels, solar cells, windmills, methane generators and other exotic equipment and parts are covered and indexed in depth.

96 pp, ill., September, 1974
LC 74-84300          $2.95

# SPICES, CONDIMENTS, TEAS, COFFEES, AND OTHER DELICACIES

FINDER'S GUIDE No. 6

*Roland Robertson*

Answers difficult questions involved with finding and purchasing unusual ingredients, beverages and foods which are difficult to obtain locally. This illustrated and indexed directory is highly browsable, to say nothing of gastronomically stimulating.

288 pp, ill., October, 1974
$3.95

# COUNTRY TOOLS

Essential Hardware and Livery

FINDER'S GUIDE No. 7

*Fred Davis*

Locates sources for the otherwise difficult to find tools essential to country living. This book covers everything from bell scrapers through goat harnesses to spoke shavers. An indispensible guide for the country resident working his land.

272 pp, ill., October, 1974
$3.95

# THE Scribner Library

America's Quality Paperback Series
## CHARLES SCRIBNER'S SONS
Shipping and Billing Departments
Vreeland Ave., Totowa, New Jersey 07512

## Order Blank

Dear Sirs:

I believe your new series "FINDER'S GUIDES" fills a definite need for information and I would like to order:

| QUANTITY | TITLE | TOTAL |
|---|---|---|
| | copies of KITS AND PLANS @ $3.95 ea. | |
| | copies of CRAFT SUPPLIES SUPERMARKET @ $3.95 ea. | |
| | copies of THE COMPLETE KITCHEN @ $2.95 ea. | |
| | copies of HOMEGROWN ENERGY @ $2.95 ea. | |
| | copies of SPICES, CONDIMENTS, TEAS, COFFEES, AND OTHER DELICACIES @ $3.95 ea. | |
| | copies of COUNTRY TOOLS @ $3.95 ea. | |
| | copies of ALL OF THE ABOVE BOOKS ($21.70 Total) | |

# NOTES